You Can't Stop Love

Restoring the World to Sanity
One Person at a Time

John Fast

ONYX PUBLISHING

First published in 2025 by Onyx Publishing, an imprint of Notebook Group Limited, Arden House, Deepdale Business Park, Bakewell, Derbyshire, DE45 1GT.

www.onyxpublishing.com
ISBN: 9781913206710

A CIP catalogue record for this book is available from the British Library.

Typeset by Onyx Publishing of Notebook Group Limited.

This book is dedicated to all the children of our world.

Addiction, Defined

A compulsive, chronic physiological or psychological need for a habit-forming substance, behaviour, or activity having harmful physical, psychological, or social effects.[1]

Ahh, the insatiable need for *more*.

Most of us, when we think of addiction (and I was once no different), conjure an image of a chronic alcoholic or drug addict who will never get enough. We believe it's the substance that's the problem. It's tangible. If someone's fix comes out of a bottle or a syringe and it's causing *harmful physical, psychological, or social effects,* then we can see it and, therefore, we can blame it.

This definition in mind, I ask you, is war an addiction? Are those who create these wars addicted to money and power? Do these actions lead to *harmful physical, psychological, or social effects*? If so, why do we keep allowing it? Is war making the world a better place? Can we continue as we have?

Is there is a solution?

---

[1] Merriam-Webster. (n.d.). Addiction. In Merriam-Webster.com dictionary. Retrieved March 4, 2024, from www.merriam-webster.com/dictionary/addiction.

Introduction

My name is Johnny, and I'm an alcoholic.

Before we go a step further, you can relax: I promise I'm not here to convince you to stop drinking. If alcohol isn't a problem in your life, why would you? Besides, as you'll come to understand, alcohol was merely a symptom of a much greater problem in my life. This little journey I wish to entertain you with is a sordid tale about not only my insanity, but the insanity that is at the helm of our world as we currently know it.

You may think a comparison between the issues related to addiction and the issues of the world at large to be a stretch, but I'm going to ask you to humour me as I invite you to look at our world from a drunk's perspective. That may seem like a bizarre request, but here is my honest opinion on the subject: the insanity that has become increasingly prevalent in our world today is no different from the insanity that I, and millions of others, once struggled with daily, at the hands of alcoholism. It is my hope that you will recognise the similarities between the dysfunction that created the need within me to drink myself into oblivion, and the insanity which lies at the root of *all* of mankind's bizarre behaviour.

That may seem to be a bold statement, but if you are open-minded enough to see the parallels between the insanity of addiction and the insanity of our wars, our racism, and the inequality that is rampant in our world, you may also see that the same, very simple solution for alcoholism may be capable of having a profound impact on every single problem mankind now faces.

One person at a time, millions of people who once suffered from the insanity of addiction have been restored to sanity, and, because of a very simple process, they've created brand-new lives. Accordingly, I ask you if it is possible for us, the people of this world, to create a brand-new society in much the same way.

If that sounds like an unobtainable, pie-in-the-sky statement, my rebuttal is simple: what else have you got? What direction are we going in? Can we, the human race, continue as we have, or must we change?

Over the years, as I've travelled the world, I've asked the people I've met these same questions, and, regardless of whether I've been in Afghanistan, India, Spain, Colombia, Cuba, the USA, or any one of a multitude of other countries, the response has been consistent. There've even been times when I've been looked at as if I were a fool for even asking, because the answer is so blatantly obvious. Race, religion, political affiliation, and economic status don't seem to have any bearing on the responses I've received. Rich or poor, black or white, liberal or conservative, we *all* seem to know that our continued existence on this planet demands some kind of transformation.

Recognising this need for change only leads to more questions. If it's so obvious that change is necessary, why do we seem stuck in a pattern of repeating the same mistakes over and over? What's holding us back? What, exactly, is it that needs to change? What will our world look like once this change has taken place? Who is ultimately responsible for changing our world?

Can we continue as we have, or must we change? This is a daunting question that many of us would rather ignore, and that may be part of the problem. Ignoring the wars, racism, inequality, and hatred that prevails in this world is exactly what has brought us to the brink. When we look closely, we discover that it is us — the people of this world — who've created every single one of the calamities which now threatens our very existence. Think about it: all our dilemmas are manmade. We've chosen to create wars and destroy the environment. We, the people, have created and participated in the very systems that support racism, inequality, and hatred.

I ask you, why? What other species would tolerate, much less create, such a self-destructive culture? Not only have our actions already led to the extinction of numerous life forms in our world, but we've also placed the future of human life itself in jeopardy. What kind of thinking allows this to take place? Are we, the most highly evolved of Earth's creatures, insane?

I'm going to ask you to pause here for a few minutes and really think about this.

I realise many of you will feel that there is nothing you, personally, can do to fix this world. Perhaps, alternatively, you feel that fixing it is not your job. Either way, I am here to tell you that you are, in fact, the *only one* who can fix it. I understand that you may feel helpless in the shadow of what appears to be an overwhelming challenge, but the good news is that you are not alone, and while this may appear to be a monumental task, it may also be much easier than you ever imagined. In fact, not only do I believe that it will be much easier than you think, but I also believe that you'll come to enjoy the ride.

Throughout history, we have employed political, economic, and military solutions for the insanity in our world, all of which have failed. Perhaps this means it is time to consider a spiritual solution. You may scoff at this, but upon close examination, and hopefully by the end of this book, you may find that the spiritual approach is not only simple, but also very practical. For the sake of argument, let's attempt to set aside our belief systems, try to be open-minded, and, at the very least, develop the willingness to examine the opportunities that the "love" option offers. After all, we *all* know, deep down inside, that love is (and always has been) the only real answer.

Who can we look to as a role model in our efforts to implement this love-based design for living? Who among us stands out as a living, breathing example of positive change rooted in love? Outside of moving to the Himalayas and joining a monastery, is there an example of an organisation with a proven, well-established track record whose members have undergone a significant spiritual (not religious) transformation and, in the process, made their homes, communities, and the world at large a kinder, more loving place?

The group people automatically turn to when trying to action any kind of societal change is the government. On the surface, this seems to be a logical choice. After all, in our democracies, our elected leaders have been entrusted with the political and economic power to create and implement policy. Why wouldn't they simply legislate an end to war, racism, and inequality? Why wouldn't they create and enforce laws that are in the best interests of the world's people? Why wouldn't they imprison corrupt officials?

Of course, we all know the answers to these questions. It's become clear that the system is broken and that our elected officials and their wealthy corporate partners have become an integral part of the problem. They have no interest in fixing the destructive system they themselves helped to design.

If we can't rely on our governments, how about the military? Well, it would be all but impossible to consider any kind of military solution. Doing so would present an inherent contradiction. How could one ever action a policy rooted in love, using force? Repeating the same mistakes over and over while expecting different results is the definition of insanity, and one would think that after a few thousand years of war and violence, we would have learned that lesson by now. This is exactly the kind of "solution" we must avoid.

We can also look to religion for examples of how to create a more loving society. But which religion? Historically, we immediately see that religious differences have been at the root of many of humanity's wars. Religion has, for some, proven to be a powerful tool in a personal context, but it has also been a very divisive force when used for political purposes. It would be unrealistic to expect the world's people to unite under a single religion.

So, our solution doesn't seem to lie with the government, the military, or religion. There is, however, a group of people which has quietly managed, on a reasonably consistent basis, to make peace with the insanity that once played an integral part in their own lives. While it was never their goal to change the world, they have accomplished exactly that. As individuals, they once arrived at a place where they desperately recognised the need for change, and they *actioned* that change. Included in their ranks are those of every race, religion, and walk of life. What they have is freely given. They have no political agenda, there are no dues or fees, and they welcome anyone who wishes to learn their way of life. Their stories of personal transformation are nothing short of miraculous, and their only goal is to help everyone and anyone who crosses their path to create a better life.

Many among them were once insane social misfits. Some were violent, and some already had one foot in the grave. Yet, motivated by a sincere willingness to be of service to their fellow man, love has, one person at a time, transformed the lives of millions of them all over the world.

The design for living they offer has been greatly effective but largely misunderstood. Perhaps the masses are not yet desperate enough to embrace the simple solution they offer, or perhaps the world's people do not fully understand the exact nature of the malady humanity faces. Either way, the reality is that we, the people of this world, stand at a turning point; a proverbial fork in the road. We can continue to rely on our trusted leaders and their massive arsenals, or we can, at the very least, examine what the love solution offers.

But what does the love solution look like in action?

On April 25, 1993, love saved me. I was thirty-seven years old, and I was knocking on death's door. I was suicidal and mentally, spiritually, and financially broke. I was essentially living to drink, and I was fully aware that alcohol was not only killing me, but also having a terribly negative impact on my family. However, on the morning of April 25, 1993, all of that changed. I woke up that morning and asked myself the most important question of my life: "Can I continue as I have, or must I change?"

This is a critical part of everything that follows, so let's stop again for a moment and clearly understand this point.

Today, over thirty years later, I fully understand that I was insane, and that booze was the medicine I was using to treat my insanity. The great misconception about addiction is that it is the substance that is the problem, but the truth is, I was far from cured once the alcohol was removed from my life; what was left was an insane man without any medicine. So, here it is in a nutshell: quitting drinking was necessary only for me to *begin* recovery. Recovery itself was all about what happened *after* I quit drinking. Recovery was about coming to terms with the root cause of my drinking: my insanity.

Recovery was also about learning, and integrating into my life, a design for living which offered me something much better than what my selfish, destructive, old way of living did. It was about developing a clear understanding of how and why I deceived others and myself; how and why I rationalised and justified my ruinous behaviour while selfishly drinking away the house payment and the grocery money. Recovery was about deciding to live with honesty, integrity, and a profound respect for the wellbeing of others. Recovery was about making better choices and embracing a design for living which allowed me to evolve into the person I truly am and always wanted to be.

For over thirty years, I've been committed to going to any length in learning how to live a happy, peaceful, productive life. Today, I am convinced that if my actions are unacceptable, the real problem lies not in the act, but in the thoughts which preceded the action.

For years, people have asked me why I still go to recovery meetings when I've not had a drink for decades. The short answer is simple: being among the beautiful souls who have loved me back to health gives me the opportunity to keep my thoughts and insanity in check. When I attend these meetings, ponder our world, and consider the fact—yes, the *fact*—that *all* of mankind's actions (the amazing and the terrible) begin with a thought, I ask: is a spiritual shift in consciousness—a spiritual "awakening"—required? Do we, must we, can we, benefit from learning how to think differently?

Now we're arriving at the crux of the matter.

If I were to select a group of people to design a manner of living for a world desperate for change, I'd stay as far away from a congressional committee as humanly possible, and I'd instead go looking for some wise old souls with several years of recovery under their belts. They not only understand change but are also committed to being of service to their fellow man. Plus, they understand the lifelong transformational process of being restored to sanity. They've lived it, and I've yet to meet a stupid alcoholic. Oh, they've done some stupid things alright, but the beautiful thing is, people in recovery are committed to learning from their mistakes, unlike those in Congress. They have realised that their continued existence on this planet relies on them letting go of their destructive ways and then developing a sincere and moral obligation to be of service to their fellow man.

How did this group of people discover such a solution?

It all started with a Wall Street banker named Bill Wilson who was on a straight road to his deathbed due to the insanity of alcoholism. He had been hospitalised on several occasions already, and the undeniable fact that he could not drink as a normal man was etched into his psyche. But that knowledge alone wasn't enough to save him. On numerous occasions, Bill would fall off the wagon and return to the bottle, with increasingly horrific consequences.

Then, in 1935, Bill was in Akron, Ohio, on a business trip. Despite being sober at the time, things weren't going well. He was agitated, and the desire to drink had returned in full force. Desperate, he called a local member of the clergy and was subsequently introduced to Dr. Bob Smith, who also suffered tremendously from the disease of alcoholism. Bill and Bob not only helped each other stay sober, but together, they went on to start Alcoholics Anonymous, which has become instrumental in transforming the lives of millions of people in almost every single country in the world.

What started as two people helping one another in their journey to sobriety has, one person at a time, blossomed into a global organisation in which millions who suffer from the insanity of addiction have been loved back to health. Each and every one of them began their recovery by clearly recognising that they could no longer continue as they had; that something had to change.

This is a very simple process, and one doesn't need to be a rocket scientist or, indeed, a drunk to grasp the fact that the world has arrived at a similar critical juncture. Feel free to call it an oversimplification, but the most appropriate analogy I can come up with to describe the actions of those in global leadership roles is that these leaders have been on one hell of a bender, and we, the people of this world, have been forced to pick up their tab. After conducting an honest appraisal of the situation, I have come to believe that it is time that we, the people, sent our trusted leaders to rehab. Do you agree?

It's difficult to put this simple message into terms that are easy for everyone to understand. A good friend in recovery once asked me, "Have you ever tried to explain alcoholism to someone who isn't an alcoholic?" and I immediately understood his point. We are all different, and yet at the same time, we are all very much alike. As a man and even as a father, I have trouble grasping what pregnancy would be like. As a Caucasian, I struggle to understand what it's like to be Asian, Black, or any other race. Let's strive to meet on a more common ground, then: being human. Let's just be human and try our very best to understand one another.

I am only one person out of over eight billion who occupy this planet. I don't have all the answers, but I believe *we*, as a collective, do. I believe that *we* can change this world. I believe this because I am acutely aware of the millions of others who have already been relieved of their own insanity and who have, in the process, become some of the most peaceful people on the planet.

Note that nothing is etched in stone. My thoughts and my experiences are merely suggestions; the beginning of a conversation which is long overdue and which we all need to have. That said, I believe the answers lie in the last place many of us are willing to look. Deep down inside, each of us has a choice in this game called life, and if humanity is going to survive, we must acknowledge and resolve the insanity which prevents us from evolving. Otherwise, we will simply continue to repeat the same mistakes over and over, until someone pushes the big red button and life as we know it comes to an end.

I have firsthand knowledge of the miracles that occur when one places love ahead of all else. Desperate and armed with the understanding that I could no longer continue as I had, I once found the courage to embrace the love offered by those who had trudged the same path as me. As a result, I've been given a brand-new life. I've been given the freedom to be who I truly am and to experience a happiness that I never knew existed. I, and millions of others, have been catapulted into a new way of life—one that no longer resembles that which I once lived and considered to be a given.

If I can do it, perhaps you can, too.

Please feel free to crack open a beer or pour yourself a glass of wine, kick back, and read on. As you will soon see, this really is a love story.

Love is the most powerful force in the world, and while we can destroy each other and this planet one hundred times over, love will still be there quietly whispering what we all know to be true: "You can't stop love."

1

What It Was Like

OUR FIRST STOP ON OUR journey is my story, since that will provide you with sufficient context to help you understand the lessons I have learned about the world and the insanity that prevails in it.

I grew up the second oldest of five children. The eldest, my brother Rick, was a year older. I was followed by two sisters — Cheryl and then Barbara — and then came Malcolm.

I didn't know this at the time, but being born into a family like mine provided me with a good start and a decent chance in life. However, life has its curveballs, and learning to hit those curveballs while embracing the lessons that accompany them can prove to be difficult, not to mention challenging. But I'm getting ahead of myself.

In my youth, home was a small village in the middle of the vast prairies of rural Saskatchewan. It's been said that Saskatchewan is so flat you can watch your dog run away for three days. We must have fed our dog too well, though, because he was always right there waiting when the school bus dropped us off every day.

As a child, I felt my life was relatively uneventful, and I remember being restless and bored by smalltown life. I was, however, a good athlete, and played baseball, football, and hockey. Unlike most of my friends, I also did a lot of things with my family: we hunted, fished, and went on family vacations. Growing up in the sixties, it was easy to develop a love of music, and I embraced Clapton, the Stones, Hendrix, and Zeppelin accordingly.

In among all of this, I was perplexed by the Vietnam War, the ongoing race issues in America, and the assassinations of JFK, MLK, and RFK. I could never understand how violence could ever be considered a viable solution to any kind of conflict.

My mother was one of the kindest, most decent human beings I have ever been blessed to have in my life. She graduated at the top of her high school class, and had she been born in a different place or time, she could have done anything she wanted. However, she grew up in a rural community during WWII and was probably unaware of her own potential and the possibilities life offered. Shortly after the war and the death of her own mother, she met my father and committed much of her life to raising her five children. She had razor-sharp wit and a great sense of humour. I learned at a young age that there was no point in lying to her because she always knew the answer before she asked the question.

Mom was no prude. She enjoyed a drink and an off-colour joke.

At two o'clock in the afternoon, it wasn't unusual to find her with her arm buried up to the elbow in a chicken's butt. By suppertime, the evidence of that chicken's delicious demise would appear on the dinner table. For years, a plaque hung in her kitchen which read, *The Opinions Expressed by The Husband In this Household Are Not Necessarily Those of The Management*, and my father, who was no pushover himself, was smart enough to never argue the point.

For six years prior to my father's retirement and my parents' subsequent move to the lake, Mom managed the local co-op grocery store. She consistently did what nobody else had before, or has since, been able to accomplish: for six years straight, she turned a profit. She was smart, capable, and hardworking, and people liked her.

Mom was also a Christian, in the *real* sense of the word: regardless of who you were, you were treated with kindness and respect. In our early years, she made sure her kids went to Sunday school, but she wasn't a Bible thumper and never pushed her beliefs onto others. She firmly believed you had to be who you were and to walk your own path.

On June 24, 1969, at the age of thirteen, life took a turn. My brother Rick and I, along with our friend Brian, stole some railroad ties and built a diving platform. We hauled it out to the local reservoir and left it a significant distance from the water so it couldn't easily be pushed in. Our plan was to return in short order with a chain and anchor and leave it close to shore.

The next day, the phone rang regarding an emergency at the reservoir. My parents and I jumped into the family car and arrived at the scene a few minutes later. We discovered that a large group of younger kids had gone for a swim. They'd managed to push the platform into the water, and when it had floated away from shore, they'd been forced to jump in and swim back.

Barbara, my little sister, hadn't made it back.

Despite my efforts over the course of the next twenty-five years to erase that moment from the hard drive of my mind, I will forever remember sitting in the back seat of that car, my mother and I clinging to each other, and my father, who was sitting in the front, turning to look at me and asking, "Why did you build the raft?"

There may be moments in everyone's life, either real or imagined, which forever alter their entire existence, and today, over fifty years after my father asked that short but powerful question, I can clearly see how my entire life pivoted in that moment. Nothing would ever be the same. Today, I can try to convince myself all day long that thirteen-year-old boys all over the world build rafts — that I was doing nothing wrong — but no amount of reasoning is ever going to fill that empty chair at the dining room table of my childhood. Nothing is ever going to fill the tremendous void in my mother's heart. Rightly or wrongly, I felt responsible for all of it.

In the same way that it is difficult to explain alcoholism to someone who isn't an alcoholic, it's equally difficult to explain what life was like following Barb's death to anyone who hasn't experienced great loss. Simply put, it decimated our family. I didn't have the skills to cope with a tragedy such as this, and travelling to the city and spending money on counselling wasn't even considered back then. You just bit the bullet and moved on. Still, nothing would ever be the same, and there was nowhere to hide. Or so I thought.

Our entire family was devastated, yet in hindsight, I can see that a firm bond between me and Mom was established that day. She bore the guilt of giving the kids permission to go swimming, and I bore the guilt of building the raft in the first place.

Barb's death crushed my mom, and she never fully got over it. To cope, she leaned into her Christian faith, and, one day at a time, she managed to put on a brave face and carry on. As best she could, she continued to take care of her family as she worked on healing. As we're about to see, I went in the other direction and worked on numbing myself and hiding from that same reality. Yet somehow, despite our going in opposite directions, she and I managed to maintain, even through the darkest of days, what may have been my only real connection with another human being at that point in my life.

For the first few weeks following Barb's death, I felt lost, and just wanted to be alone. Then, one night, a handful of the older guys took me under their wing and introduced me to alcohol — and what a beautiful thing it was. I remember being face first on the ground and hanging on for dear life as the world spun out of control. I puked everywhere. I was completely out of control, and I loved it. Afterwards, I clearly remember feeling that something wasn't quite right about it all, but that was small potatoes compared to the freedom I'd experienced.

Of course, I was totally incapable of fully processing what had happened. Still, a switch had flipped inside my brain, and the temporary relief I'd experienced from the painful reality of my life was misconstrued by my thirteen-year-old mind as a permanent solution. Overnight, booze became my medicine, and it cured a lot of ailments alright. It was magic, and from that day forward, I drank every chance I got. It's easy to look back now and see the insanity that was taking root in those moments, but back then, it was simply impossible for me to comprehend the gravity of what was taking place.

Almost immediately, the negative results of my drinking became evident. Although I had always found school boring, I had consistently managed to do reasonably well. The year following Barb's death, however, I failed my classes. I went to school for the sports, which I loved, but I really didn't give a damn about anything else.

I managed to maneuver through the next couple of years. In my last year of high school, I was the quarterback on the football team, and we kicked ass. Then, following football season, I was on the starting five on the basketball team—but only until Christmas. Following the Christmas break, I rode the bench, and I believe today that this was largely due to the impact two solid weeks of smoking and drinking had had on my physical condition.

Shortly after Christmas, Wally, our guidance counsellor and assistant football coach, stopped me in the hallway and asked me, "What are you doing here?"

"At school?" I replied, the question catching me off guard.

"There's no game. There's not even a practice today. So, what are you doing here?"

I didn't know what to say. Apparently, the teaching staff had picked up on my pattern, and Wally was putting me on the spot.

"You don't have to be here if you don't want to," he continued. "There are a number of different ways to get your education, if you really want it."

Wally had given me something to think about. School was of no interest to me. It wasn't filling the emptiness I felt inside. The only thing that came close to accomplishing that was alcohol.

I went home from school that day and never went back.

It's easy for me to sit down with others in recovery and honestly talk about who and what I became as the insanity of alcoholism took over my life. They get it. It is somewhat more difficult to explain this to the general public, perhaps because many are not used to openly discussing the level of insanity which eventually led me to recovery, nor are they used to the level of honesty those in recovery come to embrace. The hard truth is that by the time I reached seventeen years of age, I was already a full-blown alcoholic and, as a friend puts it, "You can't see it when you're in it." I *thought* I was ready for life. I *thought* I had a handle on things. I *thought* I was in control. But the fact is, the opposite was true. I was completely out of control.

When I left school, I went to work underground in a potash mine. On my days off, I partied and drank almost every dime I earned. Occasionally—usually when sporting a nasty hangover—I would hear this little voice from deep down inside whispering to me that my drinking was out of line. A few drinks would quiet that distraction, and the party would continue.

My job lasted until that summer, when the weather turned nice. I pulled into the parking lot at work one beautiful, sunny day and just couldn't find the resolve to get off the motorcycle the bank had helped me buy. I turned that motorcycle back onto the highway and rode away from the mine, the job, and the bank.

It wasn't that I didn't care. Or, at least, my line of thought wasn't as blasé or flippant as that. A more accurate assessment may be that at that point, I didn't know *how* to care. Not once did I consider the concerns of my employer or the bank manager, both of whom had been kind enough to help me out. I was incapable of seeing how self-centred I was. All that mattered was that I got what I wanted, and that left little room to consider the impact my actions were having on anyone else.

Early in my recovery, a friend stated, "Alcoholics don't get into relationships, they take hostages," and we all laughed because we all knew it was true. Later, as a recovering alcoholic, I began to see the patterns which were evident in my past. The need to control others is consistent in the lives of alcoholics, and this most certainly isn't a positive attribute when you're trying to develop healthy relationships. However, at that time, I was nowhere near recovery, and thus did not understand this aspect of my condition.

Then came the fateful day when I pulled my motorcycle up to the gas pumps a few months after ditching my mining job, to discover some girl's butt hanging out the window of the gas station kiosk.

I liked the view.

The girl—Loretta—informed me, with a smile and while

pumping my gas, that she had locked herself out.

By this point, I was eighteen and had gotten myself a new job working on a grain elevator repair crew in her hometown. I quickly discovered that Loretta also liked to party, and so, in short order, I was as addicted to her as I was to anything that came out of a bottle.

Less than a year later, I asked Loretta to marry me. I was drunk, she was drunk, and, just like my drinking, I knew deep down inside that I was making a mistake. As it turned out, I wasn't alone in this. Still, she said, "Yes."

Maybe it was a result of the long, cold winters, but it seemed customary in smalltown Saskatchewan in those days for boyfriends to get their girlfriends pregnant and then quickly marry them. While that wasn't the case in our situation, it just so happened that when Loretta did fall pregnant, her due date was exactly nine months after our wedding day. In the end, her mother was pleased that our daughter had the decency to be born two weeks late.

Sherry swept her way into my heart. While things in my and Loretta's marriage became increasingly problematic, there wasn't one single day when I didn't look forward to going home after work and having that baby on my knee. Our son, Craig, was born two years later.

I loved being a father and spent as much time as humanly possible with my kids, but by the time Craig was born, the marriage had all but disintegrated. This was tearing me up emotionally. Of course, these problems also fueled my drinking, but my denial, coupled with my ability to rationalise and justify practically anything, prevented me from seeing the truth, and I somehow managed to convince myself that none of it was my fault.

Again, I'll reiterate: you can't see it when you're in it. I couldn't see who and what I had become. I was terribly immature and very irresponsible. Nothing was ever my fault. I blamed my bosses, my neighbours, the dog, and Loretta for everything that didn't meet my expectations. I was a chronic control freak and deeply afraid of being without my kids. Being with them was the only thing that had ever offered me a shred of sanity. It was the only real love I'd ever known.

I think it's fair to say that Loretta and I both had our issues and neither of us were angels. I have no desire to bash my ex-wife. I'm ashamed to say I did enough of that while I was married to her. What I *am* trying to convey here is that because emotions tend to play a significant role in the lives of people, and because Loretta played such an integral part in my life, the repercussions of our relationship would be foundational to what happened in the years that followed. Then again, I believe that even if I'd married the most perfect woman in the world, I still would have been an insane alcoholic who would have likely destroyed the best of relationships. This automatically absolves Loretta of any blame that I convinced myself she deserved in the past.

I realise that you, the reader, are not going to think well of me for the role I played as my relationship disintegrated. You're in good company, because I didn't think well of me, either.

Through all of this and despite the insanity in my life, I continued to try and resolve things with Loretta, largely because I was so madly in love with my children. I couldn't imagine not being with them. On three different occasions, I convinced Loretta that we should try counselling, but she was never comfortable with discussing our problems or the events of her childhood with anyone, including me. Genevieve, one of the counsellors we met with, was someone I developed a solid connection with and continued to meet with on my own. Through our sessions together, I arrived at a point where I realised that the marriage was over.

I told Loretta we were done. Being the control freak I was, I packed a bag for her and asked her to leave.

It was a difficult time, but I was relieved that there had been some kind of resolution, although I wasn't pleased with the fact that it had been unilateral.

Several months passed, and Loretta occasionally saw the kids, which left me with the impression that she was reasonably content with the situation. Then, one day, I ran into her, and she told me that we were going to court over custody of the kids. When I asked why, she explained that her mother had informed her that she was out of the will if she didn't do so. I was disappointed but not surprised, and I responded to this news by filing for and receiving an interim custody order through family court.

It was a tumultuous time, and I am so grateful to my mother, who helped me so much during this time, especially with the kids.

Things gradually levelled out, and I entered a stage of my life where I was seriously happy. I met a lady named Sandy and fell in love with her, and, for reasons I will never fully comprehend, she loved me more than I will ever know. She also loved the kids.

During this time, work had been sporadic, and even though it had been nearly a decade since I'd left high school, I decided to enter a pre-law program at the local university. At the suggestion of the assistant dean, I took a full set of classes and majored in political science. This was a huge workload, but the challenge was gratefully accepted, and I worked my ass off. When I received my first set of grades at the end of the first semester, I was very pleased. Life was good. I wasn't stupid. I wasn't a failure. I had Sandy, my kids, and meaningful and challenging work. For the first time in my life, I was truly happy. Amid this came family court and, while it was rare for men to receive custody, I had no reason to not be confident.

Two days had been scheduled for the court hearing, but my reality was shattered less than thirty minutes into day one. Something was off — I could feel it — and, as I listened to my lawyer, I turned to Sandy and whispered, "We're getting screwed." By the end of the second day, I had lost all desire to become a lawyer.

Sandy and I went home and spent the next couple of months going about our lives while anxiously waiting for the decision. At the end of April, as I was preparing for my last exam, we got the news: the kids had been ordered to go live with Loretta. Sandy and I were both devastated.

I focused on my last exam, and the first stop I made when that exam was over was the liquor store.

For years, I'd had the opportunity to accept joint custody, which Loretta would have been more than happy with. The truth is, I was selfish. I wanted control. I was hurt and angry, and I wanted to teach her a lesson. The story I'd convinced myself of was that I wanted what was best for the kids, but what I know today is that I was, simply, damaged goods. I'd never healed from the loss of my sister all those years before, and everything I did was still motivated by what *I* wanted, with little regard for anyone else. I was incapable of having a real relationship with anyone and was so intent on controlling things that I couldn't see the damage I was inflicting on the other people in my life.

This means what happened next really isn't pretty.

We arranged for the kids to go live with Loretta straight away, so they could have the opportunity to meet some kids in the neighbourhood before school was over for the summer. A few short days later, I found myself getting on a plane to go to work on a remote construction project in the Canadian north. I hadn't received a paycheck in a long time, and we needed the money. As I sat on that plane waiting for boarding to finish and the door to close, I had a terrible feeling that going up into the bush with a bunch of industrial construction workers wasn't going to be a good thing, considering my mental and emotional fragility. The little voice from deep inside screamed at me to get off that plane.

I didn't listen. The circumstances that unfolded over the course of the next few days collectively formed what I consider to be one of the strangest and most regrettable events of my life.

On bigger projects in remote locations, it was common for the company to set up a bar so the guys could blow off some steam in a more controlled environment, and this project was no exception. We didn't work on Sundays, which meant those of us on the nightshift had Saturday night off. As luck would have it, our crew won a wad of cash in the Stanley Cup Hockey Pool, and, needless to say, it all got spent on booze.

At some point during the night, I went to the men's room. Sitting at a table along the way was a young lady who waved me over. She didn't say hello. She didn't introduce herself. She didn't ask for my name. She simply looked at me and muttered one of the strangest things I'd ever heard: "I just lost my son in a custody case."

I couldn't believe what I had heard. I looked at her, somewhat dumbfounded, and replied, "Fuck you. I just lost both of my kids," before turning and walking away.

I'd had a lot to drink, and her comment had rattled me. I tried to comprehend the possibility of it all being just a coincidence, but somehow, that concept was difficult to accept. How could she have known?

At closing time, as the place emptied out, I watched her leave, and then, for good measure, I waited several more minutes before I departed. As I walked out the door, I found her sitting on the step waiting for me.

I was only on that trip for two weeks, but by the time I returned home, things between me and Sandy were over. Oh, it took a while for the dust to settle, but, fueled by a belly full of booze, I'd gone to places I hated myself for, and she knew it.

It felt as though I had lost my kids, the woman I loved, and my future all at the same time.

Nothing about my response to these events was conscious. As the wreckage piled up, I became incapable of recognising and working through the events of my past. I just wanted the pain to stop. My reaction to the events I was facing at the age of twenty-seven was no different to my coping mechanism at the age of thirteen: I drank.

Insanity, as we know, is repeating the same actions over and over and expecting different results. While booze *seemed* to be the magic elixir that solved all my problems, the truth was, I only *thought* my problems were solved. In reality, they weren't. They simply piled up in the back of my mind as the tape played, constantly reminding me that the world was a cruel and ugly place and that while love may be possible for others, it was far too painful for me.

For the next decade, the slow downward spiral continued, and I literally bounced all over Canada. I was in and out of relationships, in and out of jobs, in and out of businesses, and in and out of bars. I had one job in sales which I did extremely well in, but even those successes were the result of hard drinking with clients who also had a penchant for alcohol.

The thing from this time that is the most difficult to admit is, I became a deadbeat dad. For the record, and in my own defence, I had been so confident that the children would remain with me (prior to the custody case) that Loretta and I had negotiated an agreement exempting the parent without custody from ever paying support. Thus, despite being a student with little income, I had never once asked Loretta for any support while the children had been living with me. I further justified my reluctance to pay support by rationalising that if the contents of Loretta's parents' will was the motivating force behind her bid for custody, then her parents could pay to raise the kids.

My anger had hardened into a deep-seated resentment which governed my entire thought process, and the obvious moral obligation to help and support my children was lost in the reality that I drank everything I earned, begged, borrowed, or stole. I rarely talked to my children, and months would go by between visits. What I know today is that I really didn't want them to see who and what I had become.

This may seem depressing, and it was. I remember looking at the front end of oncoming trucks as I passed them on the highway, silently fighting with myself to stay on my side of the road. In truth, I didn't really have the courage to end it all; I was afraid I would fail at suicide, too.

It's necessary for me to share this if you are to understand the insanity that was at play in my life; to grasp the full extent of the transformation that was soon to take place.

One evening during this time, I stopped at the bar on my way to my folks' place at the lake. It was a bitterly cold night as I left to travel the last few miles.

Feeling no pain, I caught a patch of ice and hit the ditch.

Fortunately, I managed to guide the car through the snow and back up onto the road, but this experience forced me to think. I was only wearing a light jacket. Had I stayed in that ditch in that remote spot and on a night that cold, too drunk to move, I would have likely either encountered a cop and spent the night in jail, or someone would have found my frozen ass the next morning.

As I slowly made my way down the road, I once again heard the little voice rising from deep inside me, whispering, "It's the drinking." I knew this was true. It was getting harder and harder to deny this.

I'm sure that my parents were completely baffled by my behaviour at this point. They were in bed when I arrived that night. I was welcomed by the dog as I let myself in. I set my six-pack on the table, opened one, and pulled up a chair. Sitting in silence, I did my best to consider my options. At some point, my dad came out and, with his typical dry sense of humour, suggested I get to bed. I then slipped into my drunk philosophical state as I once again replayed the tape of my life. I considered what my parents had gone through; what I had put them through. I thought about my children and about how chronically unhappy I'd become. I thought about my failed marriage and all the failures that had followed.

Could I continue as I had — or did something need to change?

I then considered the possibility that the *something* warranting change might just be me.

As I gazed upon the last beer in the six-pack, the thought rolled through my mind that, by the time it was finished, it would be time for me to make a decision.

At 3AM, the last empty can hit the floor, and I looked at the phone. I picked it up and called the local Drug and Alcohol Detox Centre. I had a nice chat with the person who answered, and we confirmed that I would check in the next day at 3PM. I then went to bed and had the best sleep I'd had in years.

The following morning, true to my word, I packed a bag and told my parents what I had decided to do. A few hours later, just after

3PM, I arrived at the detox and explained to the man who met me at the door that I was the guy who had called the night before.

"What guy?" he asked. I explained that I had called in the middle of the night and confirmed my arrival for this afternoon. At this, he chuckled and said, "Do you have any idea how many calls we get like that? Nobody ever actually shows up." His name was Ken, and I appreciated his candour and sense of humour. He introduced me to Michelle, who walked me through the intake procedure.

At one point during the process, I gave a flippant response to one of Michelle's questions. She paused, set her pen down, and, looking me dead in the eyes, said, "You're anti-authority, aren't you?"

Remaining consistent, I replied with a grin, "Not as long as you see things my way."

She simply nodded in acknowledgement, and we continued.

I had arrived believing that I had a problem with alcohol. What I would soon discover was that I actually suffered from a multitude of character defects typical in those of my ilk. My insolence, my self-deception, and my ability to rationalise and justify my insanity were chief among them.

What's funny is that nobody *wants* to be an alcoholic, nor does anybody *want* to be in a detox facility, yet right from the beginning, I felt I belonged there and that I was doing the right thing. There was a camaraderie, a connection, a sense of belonging, among the clientele that I had rarely, if ever, experienced before. A few days in, when Ken asked how I was doing, my honest response was, "I'm great. I can't remember ever feeling this good."

"But you're in detox," he replied, a puzzled look on his face.

"I know. I don't understand it, either."

The information I received from these wonderful people regarding the disease of addiction fit my life like a glove. Right away, I knew I was in the right place. A great deal of emphasis was placed on the need to spend time with and learn from others who had also suffered from the same insane malady. This meant going to recovery meetings and building relationships with those who had experienced a spiritual transformation and walked the same path.

On the tenth day of my residence at the detox centre, armed with my newfound knowledge, I left the facility and confidently walked out the gate. I managed to stay sober for the next thirty days. Then, my insanity once again rose to the surface. Over the course of that month, I'd gone to a couple of meetings, but I had made no real decision or commitment to change. This meant that when my anger and resentment toward the past boiled over one night following a bitter argument with Loretta, I went out and got obliterated.

From that point, I pretty much stayed drunk for the next six months.

There is a saying that "recovery will ruin your drinking", and let me tell you, nothing could be more accurate. I had admitted to my friends, family, and the innermost part of myself that I had a problem with alcohol. So, while the insanity ran rampant in my life over those six months, that little voice grew louder and louder with every drink I had. I could no longer blame anyone for my actions. There was no justification for this. *I* was the problem.

There is nothing that could compare to the misery of those six months as I hid from the world, submerged in an ocean of liquor, with only one goal in mind: to stay medicated.

An old rancher once offered me a pearl of wisdom, and it has passed every litmus test I've ever put it through. "Nothing," Russell said, "goes in a straight line forever." I honestly believed that the path I was walking was heading straight to the cemetery. Then, early one morning during this period, my phone rang.

"Can we go for lunch?" my daughter Sherry asked.

It had been a while since I had seen her, largely because I had been attempting to distance myself from everyone. She was now sixteen, and my initial inclination was to say no. I thought she might want money, and I didn't want anyone dipping into my already-slim drinking budget. Nonetheless, I agreed to come, despite my disappointment when she picked a relatively expensive restaurant as our meeting place.

It was a quiet get-together; neither of us was predisposed to babbling. In the middle of our meal, Sherry said, "There's something I need to tell you."

"What?"

"Never mind."

"What is it?"

"Forget it," she said.

I don't know where it came from, but what fell out of my mouth next was, "You pregnant?"

Sherry looked down at the table and asked, "Will you tell Mom?"

Telling Loretta wasn't difficult. I knew she and Sherry had been butting heads for a long time, and Sherry wanted to avoid the confrontation. Even still, Loretta needed to know, and she handled it in much the same way she had dealt with every issue that we'd ever come up against: she didn't say a word and simply turned, walked into her bedroom, and closed the door.

I let myself out.

For the next eight days, I drank and sifted through my past. It had been almost ten years to the day since my children had gone to live with Loretta, and the anger I'd held toward her, her parents, and my lawyer at that time was still fresh in my memory. At this acknowledgement, a question, small but powerful, welled up from deep down inside me: *Isn't ten years enough?* And then another: *What kind of grandpa do you want to be?* That second question gave me pause and led to what people in recovery refer to as a "moment of clarity". Suddenly, I began to see things from an entirely different perspective. The truth I could no longer deny was that *I* was the one pouring the booze down my throat. Yes, others had played some negative roles in my life, but I could clearly see that my response to everything negative I'd ever gone through — from the death of my sister, to lost high school football games, to failed relationships — had been to get, and stay, thoroughly intoxicated. How could I blame anyone else for that?

For the first time in my life, I looked honestly at my own behaviour, and I came to see that I was not only destroying my own life, but that my actions had had a negative impact on the lives of all those I professed to love. I realised, in short, that my children, my parents, my friends, Sandy, and Loretta had all paid the price for my inability to deal with the reality of my life. Through that small crack, I caught a glimpse of how angry, selfish, and destructive my thought process had been.

I began to consider the possibility that maybe, just maybe, I had been wrong about so many things. So very many things.

Somewhere during that moment of clarity, I made a decision. I had failed as a father; the wreckage was too great for me to sugarcoat it any other way. Becoming a grandfather, however, offered me a shot at redemption. If I was going to be a grandfather, I wanted to be the best grandpa I could possibly be.

The truth had hit me in the face, and I could no longer deny it. I called the detox and checked in the very next morning.

2

What Happened

"WHAT ARE YOU DOING BACK here?" Ken asked, breaking into a grin as I walked through the door.

"I had a fight with my ex-wife," I replied, suddenly realising how ridiculous that sounded.

"Well, you sure showed her, didn't you?"

I hated his grin, but I couldn't argue with him. My response to every single problem I'd ever encountered had led me back to this place. I didn't know how to live without self-destruction. It had really become that simple.

Once again, I went through the intake process, but this time was different. It was humbling. The cocky responses I had given during my previous visit were gone, and the little I had learned then had taken root. I knew, plain and simple, that I didn't have any of the answers. All I knew for sure was that doing things my way didn't work. If I wanted to survive and become the world's greatest grandpa, I had to find another way. My daughter had given me something to live for, and I spent much of that first day going over my options. "If we keep doing what we've been doing, we'll keep getting what we've been getting," someone I knew had once said. My problem was, I didn't know how to do things differently. I felt like I had run out of options. There was no Plan B. So, then and there, regardless of how unpalatable it felt, I surrendered. I decided that I was going to put "doing things my way" on the shelf and do whatever these people suggested to the very best of my ability, no matter what transpired.

Later that afternoon, I ran into Ken again outside on the deck. I told him about my daughter and the struggles I'd experienced since my last visit. "You're a long way off your path," he pointed out. "Why don't you try praying?"

"Praying?" I echoed as the hair stood up on the back of my neck. "To what?"

"It doesn't matter. Just get on your knees and start talking."

I opened my mouth to argue, but then just as quickly realized there was nothing I could say in response. It had only been a couple of hours since I'd promised myself that I was going to do whatever these good people suggested. This was my first test. Had I meant it? Did I really want to be the world's greatest grandpa? Was there another choice? Was there any other option? The answers were obvious. I buttoned my piehole and walked away.

I mulled all of this over and examined my beliefs. My studies had consistently revealed that religion was used all too often as a political tool and had historically been a major factor in a long list of wars—wars that had led to the deaths of millions of people.

I thought about my college history professor, a brilliant man who had once been an Anglican minister in the UK before coming to his senses and leaving the church. I thought about the history of sexual abuse within the Catholic church and its involvement in the residential school fiasco in Canada that continues to this day.

But then I realised Ken hadn't said anything about religion. In my limited discussions with others, I had been told that there was a *spiritual* (not religious) aspect to the recovery process, and that participants were encouraged to develop a personal relationship with a Power greater than themselves—a God *of their own understanding*. The lines were blurry, and I wasn't sure what it all meant, but Ken's words stuck in my head: *It doesn't matter. Just get on your knees and start talking.*

I slept well that night. The next morning, I negotiated my way from the coffee pot, through the clientele, and out the back door. I was grateful to be alone and for the opportunity to survey my surroundings. I climbed the back staircase and took a seat on a step near the top, where I was offered the best view.

I was confused. I didn't know how to proceed. I sat there trying to make sense of things, and I asked myself, "What am I going to pray to?"

I took a few minutes to allow myself to soak up my surroundings. It was spring, and the leaves were struggling to introduce themselves following the long, cold winter. There were a few birds about and the sun was just beginning to rise in the eastern sky. Slowly, I came to see the unique beauty in what to many may have seemed like just another day. From my vantage point, it was almost as if I was seeing the world for the first time. In fact, I couldn't remember the last time I had watched — *really* watched — a sunrise. I drank in the beauty of all I could see and feel, and the world began to look like a gigantic, beautifully crafted Swiss watch. There was an unmistakable rhythm to it all: the sun rose, announcing the coming day, at a very predictable time; the birds that had flown south months earlier had returned; the winter's snow had been chased away by the warmth of spring. This same pattern had repeated itself for millions of years. The power of the universe had nudged the sun over the horizon since time had begun. Had that power ever once taken a day off, humanity would have been finished.

I reasoned that anything that powerful might well be worth praying to.

I was clumsy and uncertain, and I had no idea how to begin, but I threw caution to the wind and began by simply asking the Power (as I had already started to think of it) — the Power that had brought the sun up every day for eternity — to relieve me of my insanity and take away my obsession with alcohol.

Would it work? I had no idea. I was only doing it because I had promised myself that I would do whatever these good people had told me to. The only things I knew with any certainty were that I could no longer continue as I had, that I really wanted to change, and that I really wanted to be the world's greatest grandpa. Having been given a glimpse of the natural perfection that existed in our world, it became clear to me that the only thing that negatively impacted the precision of this world was when man — more specifically, *this* man — *thought* he had a better way.

I was suddenly exhausted. I felt as though I had been fighting against the entire world for much of my life.

I surrendered to this Power, repeatedly asking that the obsession that had driven me to place alcohol ahead of everything else in my life be removed.

A few minutes later, I felt sapped, but satisfied with the progress I had made. I came down from my perch and went back inside. I felt decidedly different. Now that the ice had been broken, I decided I would, throughout the day, ask either out loud or within the confines of my own mind that the Power take away my obsession with alcohol. I wasn't leaving anything to chance.

Every morning for the next ten days, I filled my coffee cup and headed up the back stairs where, with new eyes, I took in the beauty of our world and asked the Power that brought up the sun to relieve me of my desire to drink. After this daily ritual, my days were filled with group discussions regarding the insanity of addiction, and specifically how to manage the thought process that could lead us back to the insanity of the bottle. The thought, after all, preceded the action.

One of my most memorable moments from this time came when Bill, the director of the facility, spoke to us regarding our futures. "For those caught in the trap of addiction, there are only three options: we can be institutionalised and spend our lives in prison or a mental hospital; we can end up in a grave; or we can end up in recovery. Those are your choices. There are no other options." As I listened to Bill, his words resonated deep within me, and my soul acknowledged what it heard to be true. I knew where I was heading and what the outcome would be if I allowed the insanity to continue to run my life. While there was a sense of familiarity that drew me back to the habits of my past, I also fully understood, for the very first time in my life, that I couldn't continue as I had. I also understood that this new path offered, at the very least, a chance of a better life.

On my last day at the detox, following my morning prayer, I came down the stairs and I packed my things. I said my goodbyes to the beautiful souls who had been so supportive during my stay, and I headed out the door. It had been a safe environment, and I was acutely aware of how afraid I was to leave.

And then a miracle—the first of many—happened. As I walked through the gate, I continued to whisper my prayer to myself, and, as the gate *clank*ed shut behind me, the sound was accompanied by a feeling unlike anything I'd ever experienced before, or even since. The message was unmistakably clear: it was not that I would *never, ever* drink again, but that I would *always have a choice.*

I was in awe. Tears rolled down my cheeks. My fear was suddenly replaced by a sense of calm and a peace I had never known before. I stood on that sidewalk for a few moments soaking it all in. For the first time in my life, I felt free.

I then tossed my bags in the car and went to see my kids.

If I were asked what the difference was between my first trip to the detox centre and my second, the answer would be simple: the first time, I received an education, and the second time, I made a decision. Wanting to change is nothing more than wishful thinking. Making a decision to go to any lengths necessary to change is a commitment.

My love for my family, children, and future granddaughter had opened my heart. Accordingly, armed with the understanding that I could no longer continue as I had, I became willing to do whatever was necessary to heal myself and to be of service to those I loved.

The stated goal of my recovery program is to encourage those who suffer from the insanity of addiction to "embrace the spiritual design for living that encourages participants to develop a relationship with a Power greater than ourselves". This goal has formed the foundation of my new life.

I will never be able to sufficiently thank the staff at the Larsen House Detox Facility for giving me a place to go, and for their love and support, in those early days. I honestly have no idea if I would be sitting here today sharing this story with you had it not been for them.

For the first while, sober life was a strange, uncertain world. I felt as though I was living in no man's land; a place in between where I'd been and where I was going.

I knew I needed to change, but I didn't understand the process that would take place during that journey. How could I? Sobriety and the spiritual way of life I was being taught to embrace were both foreign territories, and just a bit bewildering. I was thirty-seven years old, and I felt as though I was learning to live all over again—or, perhaps more accurately, that I was finally learning how to live for the first time.

While I didn't always understand what the right thing to do was, I was certainly convinced that my old way didn't work, so there would be no going back. Courtesy of my experience at the detox centre gate, I finally understood that I had that choice; that I could change.

The folks at the detox had told me to go to meetings, and this time, I actually listened. For the first time in my life, I was doing what I had been told to do. Around this time, I also reconnected with a few people from my past who I knew didn't drink and had "coincidentally" (I'll let you decide) reappeared in my life. They took me under their wing, and I am so thankful for their love and support.

As Ken had said, I was a long way off my path. I was broken mentally, spiritually, and financially. I really had nowhere else to go, so I went to stay with my parents at the lake. I will be forever grateful for their help and understanding as I worked through the issues I had been confronted with. The solitude offered by long walks along the shore and through the surrounding forest with Jiggs, my dad's crazy springer spaniel, helped immensely, and I began going to nearby recovery meetings.

I'd always thought that the people in recovery would be the most boring specimens of humanity that one could ever associate with and that I would never have fun again once I started going to the meetings. I couldn't have been more wrong. The people I met were real, tremendously courageous, and a joy to be with. They weren't afraid to speak honestly about the insanity that had been so pervasive in their own lives. As I listened and learned, it didn't take long for me to realise that there were many in this world who had suffered much greater tragedies than I had.

Early in my drinking years, I had met some individuals who, when under the influence of drugs or alcohol, were absolutely hilarious, so I can't begin to tell you how pleased I was to discover that some of my new *sober* friends were just plain nuts and some of the funniest people I had ever met. After being stuck in my own misery for a couple of decades, it dawned on me that it had been years since I had really laughed; *truly* laughed, from the pit of my stomach. I began to look forward to those meetings for no other reason than the fact that my new friends were actually fun and, what's more, had acquired a genuine sense of humility by learning to laugh at themselves. More than anything else, I was truly grateful to know there were others like me and that I was no longer alone.

I had to face the fact that my drinking was nothing more than a coping mechanism I used to keep myself emotionally numb. This numbness had prevented me from dealing with the truth and reality of my life. Stuffing the pain hadn't resolved anything. In fact, in so doing, I had also avoided the benefits that come with the healing process. As the emotional pain following Barb's death quickly resurfaced once the numbing effect of the alcohol was out of the way, I came to see that there are no shortcuts in life and that the only real way to deal with life is to have the honesty and courage to see, accept, and feel the truth.

As I sifted through the wreckage of my past, I came to learn a great deal about myself and the world I lived in. I came to realise that there was nothing I could do to change the painful events of my past and that my drinking had denied me the opportunity to learn the lessons offered by those experiences. I also came to believe that pain was an unavoidable part of life, and that the desire to numb myself to avoid it had also, unwittingly, deprived me of the ability to feel any real joy and happiness.

It slowly became clear to me that pain is a great teacher. I started to place real value in the lessons offered by the difficult times, and in turn, my fear of pain dissipated and my optimism grew.

Healing from Barb's death and the guilt attached to it was my top priority, and Mom, with the best of intentions, began to gently twist my arm to get me to go back to church. I was reluctant. My experiences sitting with real people and hearing the stories of those who had completely turned their lives around were much more powerful to me than anything I had ever experienced in church. I preferred the honest, sometimes painful, and often hilarious accounts of those who had lived as insanely as I had.

Conducting an honest appraisal of my life was difficult and painful, and yet one of the most rewarding things I've ever done. The analogy often referred to in our meetings was that of "peeling the onion", and, indeed, some tears were shed as, one by one, the layers were peeled off and I began to embrace the reality of who and what I was. I came to see that Ken had been right: I was a long way off my path. I had become unteachable. All I had to do was look back at the decade that had passed since I'd left college to verify that fact.

As I healed, my love for books was rekindled. *Tuesdays with Morrie* by Mitch Albom is a true account of the author's visits with his favourite college professor, who was dying from Lou Gehrig's disease at the time. At one point, Morrie explains that he's a "Heinz 57 kind of guy" who borrows from the teachings of Muslims, Hindus, Buddhists, Christians, and a host of other religions. I smiled when I read this. Why would I want to limit myself to one particular school of thought when there were literally thousands of different perspectives all claiming the path to God? I didn't really believe any of them to be the "correct" one, but I thought it would be prudent to remain open-minded and, like Morrie, to embrace what spoke to my heart and soul as I put together the pieces of my own life.

One ideology which appealed to me (and continues to do so) was the spirituality offered by the numerous Indigenous people I came to meet during my time in recovery. The more I learned from them, the more I came to love the impact my new friends were having on my life. The sign in the meeting room read, *Religion is for people who fear Hell. Spirituality is for people who've already been to Hell and don't want to go back.*

As I began to write about my experience in recovery and my global travels, my mom became very supportive of the message I was trying to share with others. At one point, after reading something I had written, she looked at me and said, "You know, I've been pushing you to come to church, but I'm not going to bring it up anymore. I think you're doing just fine."

I began to learn that recovery was about so much more than

merely quitting drinking. My disease had isolated me from society, and the loneliness I'd experienced had impacted my self-esteem, yet that same disease had also made me think that I was always right. When I heard someone say that alcoholics are "egomaniacs with inferiority complexes", I realised the description fit like a glove.

In one of my very first meetings, I heard an old-timer explain the insanity that is consistent in the lives of alcoholics as follows:

> We were motivated by fear, selfishness, and a need to control people, places, and things. This fear, selfishness, and the need to control others is a function of our egos. As alcoholics, we could never get enough of what we thought we wanted, and our egos consistently told us a story which rationalised and justified all our insane actions in our pursuit of more. We consistently demanded more money, more sex, more love, more control, more power, and more attention as we alienated ourselves from the people in our lives. We thought the world should run according to our agenda, and we were never satisfied with what we had. When our incomprehensible demands were not met, we became demoralised and angry, and we drank.
>
> The problem then snowballed. As our lives spiralled out of control and friends and family began to take note of our dilemma, we stood defiant and blamed others for the mess we had created. The more we drank to overcome our isolation, the greater the distance

between ourselves and others became, and the more booze it took to fill the emptiness. It wasn't only killing us; it was also destroying the lives of our families and our friends as they watched us slip into the abyss.

I was sitting in a room full of people I had barely met, but as I listened, I knew they were talking about me. I so clearly identified with everything that was being said. As the speaker accurately described me, my life, and the thought process which had repeatedly had me responding to life's difficulties in an insane manner, I surveyed the room and noticed others nodding in agreement. I was no longer alone.

Once again, I recalled Bill's words at the detox regarding the limited choices offered by the disease of addiction: an institution, a grave, or recovery. It became obvious that if I really wanted to become the world's greatest grandpa, I needed to replace the insanity in my life with something capable of filling the emptiness inside of me, while satisfying my insatiable need for *more*. Again, it was suggested that a spiritual experience (a shift in consciousness) may be the only thing capable of meeting those requirements. It was also suggested that I should take what appealed to me and leave the rest. Perhaps some of the others in the room needed to hear the messages I didn't necessarily agree with; I wasn't the only one in the room, after all.

While I was free to believe whatever I wished, I was once again reminded that "God" was a generic term and that we all had the right to develop our own understanding, based on our own beliefs, of what "God" is. What was important for me to remember was that

I wasn't God. *I* wasn't in charge. It was humbling for me to accept that my attempts at controlling my own life, never mind the universe, had won me a ticket to the local detox centre.

I recalled Ken's suggestion regarding prayer and the miracle I had personally experienced when walking out the gate. The latter had come about only after I'd petitioned the Power of the Universe, during my first attempts at prayer, on the back stairs of the detox. The other thing that helped me to embrace spirituality was the fact that the people who surrounded me in these meetings looked at the world in a similar way to me. They may have talked about spiritual matters, but they sure as hell weren't saints, Bible thumpers, or religious fanatics. I began to feel quite comfortable in their midst.

For the first few months following the detox, I focused on being sober. I quickly learned, however, that being sober wasn't enough. If I wanted to be the world's greatest grandpa, I needed to be happy doing it. What recovery offered was an opportunity to address the real, underlying issue; the insanity rooted in my ego that had created the need for me to drink in the first place. After all, a sane person would never have embraced the slow, destructive, and painful process of suicide offered by drinking yourself to death in response to past trauma.

My personal traumas had deep roots, and the entire trajectory of my life had changed dramatically due to the events of a single day. During my healing journey, I came to understand that there had been no intent on my part to hurt anyone and that there was nothing I could do to change the past. It was therefore pointless to continually punish myself for my sister's death by destroying any hope of happiness I may have ever had. Besides, I'd already done just that for nearly twenty-five years. Wasn't that enough?

One of the greatest gifts I was given in recovery was also one of the most difficult to embrace: it involved an honest and thorough self-examination of my life, with a goal of clearly seeing and accepting my role in all the issues that had caused me problems. I was encouraged to go back through my life and honestly look at the truth. I had to honestly accept where I'd been in the wrong and where my thoughts and actions had harmed others. What had motivated me to behave as I had? What need was being fulfilled within me as I demanded that the world march to my tune?

This would have been a pointless exercise if I'd simply tried to convince myself that my thoughts and actions were someone else's fault. The facts were, nobody else had poured the booze down my throat. I had frequently driven drunk, and I was the one who'd shown up to work drunk many times. I couldn't blame anyone else for the fact that I, and I alone, had made booze the biggest priority in my life. My recovery therefore depended upon my willingness to be rigorously honest in my search for the truth.

This was a difficult process, but nothing has ever been so rewarding. We are what we do, and this process gave me a great deal of insight into who I had become and what, exactly, needed to change. I was able to clearly see what worked, what didn't, what made me happy, and what fueled the insanity. I began to stop blaming others and to honestly own what I had done.

My initial attempts at this were superficial, but I didn't have to go very deep to see the consistent patterns. I could see how my behaviour had impacted my marriage, work, and relationships with friends and family. I came to clearly see that drinking itself was my insane response to many of the painful issues in my life, going back as far as the death of my sister.

None of this was an overnight matter. If it had been as simple as just quitting drinking, all my problems would have been dealt with instantly. But as I listened to and identified with the stories of others, I began to see that true recovery was about so much more than simply quitting drinking; it also offered a design for living that was much better than anything I'd ever encountered before.

I began to experience real hope in my life. I had arrived at recovery with what I thought was a long list of problems, but, one by one, things began to work themselves out as I quit trying to control everything and everyone and began to simply focus on helping others whenever possible (and enjoying the ride).

Eight months after my last drink, my beautiful granddaughter, Delicia, was born, and I wept. She and I have grown up together. I am also now a great-grandfather, as Delicia and her husband, Tyson, are the proud parents of two beautiful little girls, with another baby on the way. Of course, I immediately accepted the challenge of becoming the world's greatest great-grandfather. Not to be outdone, my son, Craig, and his partner, Michelle, decided to also get in on the act, and have blessed the family with a beautiful baby boy.

The miracles keep on coming.

By the time a few years had passed, I was living a life I had never imagined. My social life was primarily focused on events within the recovery community, and wherever we went and whatever we did, laughter followed.

There was a day when ten or twelve of us met for lunch, and there at the next table sat a group representing the local chapter of Hell's Angels. At one point, I excused myself to go to the restroom, and, upon my return, I paused around the corner, out of sight, and just listened to the noise and laughter coming from my group. Had you painted this scenario before I'd met my new friends, I would have naturally assumed that it was the bikers who were taking the place apart, but it was actually the band of sober social misfits who were responsible for all the racket. "Boring" wasn't in their vocabulary. What they were was *real*. It's often said that alcoholics stop maturing emotionally when they start drinking, and I've often wondered if they revert to that age when they sober up. These guys seemed to be living their new lives like a band of forty- or fifty-year-old teenagers. They were having fun, and I realised that some of that may have rubbed off on me.

My new friends included judges, lawyers, policemen, salesmen, and people who had done time for murder. I'm pleased to say that I've sat in meetings with recovering alcoholics who were white, brown, Muslim, atheist, gay, Hindu, Asian, and Native North American. Some were millionaires and some were barely scraping by. Some were well-educated, some weren't, and some had gone back to school and earned degrees. Everyone had one thing in common: they were all welcome. Nobody was turned away.

Recovery had provided millions of people from all over the world with a second chance to become the person they really were, before their insanity had taken them in a different direction. Recovery offered a safe place for me to go to and safe people for me to be with. The loneliness of my drinking days vanished as I continued to go to several meetings a week.

By this time, I'd learned and embraced a few spiritual principles which I'd tried to incorporate into my life. Through this process, I came to believe that there is no such thing as a coincidence; that everything happens for a reason. That made sense to me. Life was about balance. I wasn't a doormat, but neither was it my job to control the world and its people. I'd surrendered, done my best to stop fighting the things I couldn't control, and simply focused on accepting life as it was and keeping my side of the street clean. Life was good as a result.

In 2005, as I was closing in on twelve years of sobriety, my telephone rang out of the blue, and a nice lady on the other end asked me, "Would you like to come to work in Yemen?"

By this time, I had begun to enjoy waking up in the morning with a clear head. My fear of change had become much more manageable, and not only had I become content with my new design for living, but I also really couldn't imagine having it any other way.

I had consistently turned down work opportunities that would make it difficult for me to attend recovery meetings, simply because the people in recovery had become such an integral part of my life. Yemen, however, was a different kettle of fish, and the little voice inside told me I needed to pay attention. I considered that Yemen, being a Muslim country, would likely be alcohol-free.

If I accepted the position, my first trip would be seven weeks long — a long time when you have no idea what you're getting into. I also had some angst regarding the stability of the region. My interest in politics from my college days had continued, and I knew the media reports on Yemen hadn't painted a pretty picture.

I talked the situation over with a gentleman I knew who had worked in Yemen, and in doing so, I developed a better understanding of the place. I then sat quietly and listened out for the little voice inside.

Early in my sobriety, I had experienced some anxiety regarding my future. I'd talked this over with my good friend Bill, explaining that I felt as though I were standing on the edge of a cliff. I knew I couldn't go back, but I was afraid to take the next step forward. Bill had smiled and said, "That's why we're here. Go ahead. Take the step. We'll catch you." This situation wasn't much different. All I had to do was trust what the universe was putting in my lap.

I stepped off that cliff, and Yemen changed my life forever.

3

A New Perspective

MY ARRIVAL IN YEMEN WAS far from graceful. In fact, the flight there was the worst stint of travelling I'd ever done, and I'll do my best to never get on a KLM flight again. I landed in Sana'a frustrated, exhausted, and a full twenty-four hours late, and I *still* had one more connecting flight to make.

The airport terminal was right out of Casablanca: it was small, old, and dark, and smelled of a million past cigarettes. For whatever reason, all arriving baggage was put through an X-ray machine, and as my bags came out the other end, a small, older man, his cheek bulging with khat, quickly grabbed my bag, dragged it across the terminal floor, and dropped it in front of the counter of my connecting flight. He then stepped between me and the bag and, flashing a mouthful of brown teeth, stuck his hand out and said, "Fifty dollars."

I stopped and surveyed the small group of amused men who were watching the events unfold. I wasn't in the mood for a shakedown, but I also realised I was alone and on their turf. I pulled twenty dollars out of my pocket and handed it to him. I then reached down to get my bag, but he stuck his hand out, demanding more. I stopped, looked him in the eye, and simply shook my head and said, "No." I then looked at his friends to make sure they all understood the message. I grabbed my bag and finished checking in. My flight was already boarding, and I had no desire to spend the night in this place.

The Yemini Airways plane was filthy and didn't smell any better than the airport. I sat back and stared out the window as the green fields surrounding Sana'a gradually gave way to mountains and desert.

The flight took about an hour, and we landed at Riyan Airport, where the terminal was big, bright, and new. There were no other Caucasian men on the flight and there were few in the airport, so it wasn't difficult for my driver to find me. He spoke no English and was accompanied by a military escort who brandished an AK-47. I would later be told that the escort was there to provide security, and the story, thankfully unsupported by any obvious evidence, was that if anything happened to me, he would be shot.

We climbed into a Toyota Land Cruiser and began our journey to the base camp in the Masila Oilfield. As we travelled, it didn't take more than a few minutes for me to realise that this was a different world. Actually, it was two very different worlds. There was the world of the new airport, the wide new highways, and the number of fine vehicles, all of which indicated that there was significant wealth in this nation. This, however, contrasted greatly with the other world, where hovels served as homes and dilapidated fruit stands posed as the centres of commerce. The greatest indication that extreme poverty was well-rooted within this society was the gaunt and hopeless countenance of the beleaguered pedestrians we passed.

The trip had been long and hard, and as I stared back at those faces, I wondered what I had gotten myself into.

As the driver raced the Land Cruiser across the Yemen desert, the escort drifted in and out of sleep. His AK, resting by his side, was jostled by the movements of the vehicle and came to rest pointing directly at my head. I slumped to the other side of the car and drifted off myself.

Upon my arrival, I met Terry, the site superintendent. He had Peter, the clerk, arrange my lodging, and one by one, I met the other supervisors. There were a few from the UK and a couple of other Canadians. I unpacked and turned in early, hoping to catch up on some sleep, but that plan didn't go well: I slept poorly. I chalked it up to jetlag. By the next morning, I'd reasoned that it may take me a few days to adjust to my new surroundings.

I had come in a week early so Dave, the supervisor who I would be taking over for at the end of the week, could show me around and introduce me to the job and crew. The Masila Oilfield was roughly five hundred square miles in size, and it contained approximately one thousand oil wells. My crew was responsible for all the electrical construction and maintenance work associated with the operation. We had several different projects on the go, and my job was to oversee these activities and make sure my crew had what they needed to do their job safely.

The Masila Oilfield was in the Hadramout region of Yemen, and to this day, I think of it as one of the most beautiful places I've ever seen. Massive wadis, some one thousand feet deep, wound their way through the entire area. I was amazed that you could be easily within eyesight of a particular wellsite, but because of the terrain, it would be a fifty-mile drive to get there. The experience seemed biblical, and I chuckled to myself as I thought of Charlton Heston stepping out from behind a boulder carrying two stone tablets.

A few days later, Dave left me to fend for myself. There was a lot to learn, but I'd been in those situations before, so that wasn't an issue. What *was* an issue was my anxiety. I still wasn't sleeping well, and the less I slept, the more anxious I became. I just couldn't seem to relax, and, in this isolated corner of the world, I didn't know what to do about it.

When I realised that I had been there for over a week and still hadn't had a bowel movement, I began to get concerned. What the hell was wrong with me? The process of self-examination that I'd been taught in recovery prompted me to quiet my mind and ask myself some very pointed questions, beginning with, "What, exactly, am I feeling?" The response which resonated from within me was immediate: *Fear!* This naturally invited the next question: "What are you afraid of?" A second, maybe two, passed, and then I heard the answer, loud and clear: *I'm afraid all the people here want to kill me.* "Is my fear real, or is it imagined?" I asked myself. To answer that question, I began to pay close attention to the people around me, and it only took a couple of days for me to conclude that the local Yemeni people meant me no harm. I could see that there was always the possibility of a desperate attempt to take a white Canadian citizen hostage, but I viewed that as an economic issue, not an act of terrorism.

My fear diminished, and I struggled to imagine how these poor souls could ever realistically be viewed as a real threat to the military forces of any western nation. This in mind, I wondered where my fear had actually come from. After all, it had caused real anxiety — anxiety which had threatened my physical health — so I wanted to know and understand where the belief that "all these people want to kill me" had come from.

As I have mentioned, it was 2005. Following 9/11 and the invasions of Afghanistan and then Iraq, I was intrigued by the possibility that the western media, which I had consumed for years to "stay informed", had somehow convinced me that the entire Muslim world was a threat to my existence. If so, I was somewhat embarrassed that I had allowed myself to be indoctrinated in such a manner. Then again, the mainstream media, I reasoned, wouldn't have gone to all this trouble just for little old me. I began to wonder if the entire western world had been taken for a walk by the American media to garner support for these wars.

My thoughts turned to my daughter, Sherry, who had graduated with a degree in international studies and given me a great book called *Confessions of an Economic Hit Man*, in which author John Perkins explains, in detail, the foreign policy strategy created by the corporate and political leadership of the United States.

Perkins himself had been an "economic hitman". Vetted by the National Security Agency, his job was to convince the leadership of countries which were either strategically important to the USA or rich in natural resources (such as oil) to accept massive infrastructure loans for developments within their respective nations. These loans, typically from the World Bank or the IMF, were guaranteed by the government of the United States. This guarantee ensured that major American corporations would be designing and building these projects and making billions in the process. Once burdened with debt, these nations ultimately faced the reality that the promised increase in GDP would not be sufficient to repay the loans. In danger of defaulting, they then fell under the economic control of the United States government and other US-dominated agencies. These parties used the debt as leverage to politically manipulate and economically control the nation's natural resources.

I had only been in Yemen for a few days, and I wasn't convinced of anything yet. I certainly didn't want to jump to any conclusions. At the same time, I couldn't deny what I was witnessing. The pieces of the puzzle were falling into place, and the scenario described by Perkins began to make sense to me.

That night, I slept. A calmer, more relaxed version of me showed up for work the next morning, and I began to get to know my crew. My behaviour during the first couple of weeks had been mired in anxiety and largely based on the information I had been provided with during my first week spent with Dave. But my assessment of the men I was supervising started, in very short order, to directly contradict the version Dave had provided me with. The men who worked for me were primarily from India, and they were capable, committed, and extremely knowledgeable. In addition to their capabilities on the job, I began to see how kind, peaceful, and respectful they were.

Over those first few weeks, things went smoothly — well, apart from a bit of insanity created by a couple of superintendents who had the propensity to become belligerent on a belly full of booze. The government of Yemen, while devoutly Muslim, had decided to look the other way when it came to expats who worked there bringing in alcohol. The drinking didn't bother me, and most of the guys would only have a few drinks and a few laughs. But there was a small group of hardcore drunks who would frequently get abusive — which simply added another layer of difficulty to an already difficult situation. It was suggested to me that any important discussions with Steve were better left until the afternoon, so he could first negotiate his way through the worst part of his daily hangover. It didn't take long for me to discover that avoiding him altogether was an even better strategy.

As I neared the end of that first trip, there was a moment — a moment which reminded me of my experience at the detox gate — that I will never forget. I was out in the middle of the beautiful Yemen desert when a powerful thought seemingly came out of nowhere and hit me like a brick: *What I am seeing with my own two eyes doesn't match the story we've been told.* I stopped and wondered, why was there this discrepancy? Most of the local people here were struggling to survive and were incapable of mounting any kind of real threat against the west. This contradicted North American media reports. I had to ask myself, why the deception? I sat there for a long time, processing the experience of the past few weeks. The foreign policy pattern Perkins described in his book had been revealed right in front of me. That part was obvious. What's more, I also began to recognise some similarities from my own personal past.

Alcoholics, when drinking, are a dishonest lot. Their addiction creates the need to manipulate and deceive others. They're selfish. They often don't care about anyone else and will do anything to get what they want. Nothing is ever their fault. Ultimately, they also deceive themselves and become convinced of their own nonsensical stories. Their selfishness makes doing the right thing and being responsible all but impossible.

I wondered if it was only because I had lived with my own alcohol-induced self-deception for so long that I was able to recognise these same character defects in other situations. "You can't con a con," the old guys in recovery had told me – another lesson I'd come to be grateful for.

It had only been through the process of becoming rigorously honest and developing the courage to fearlessly examine my own life that I had been able to change and escape the self-deception created by my own ego. And now, standing in the Yemen desert, I began sorting through my beliefs regarding the world we lived in using that same process. Many of my beliefs had been based on the *story* we'd been told by the western media, and now I found myself seriously doubting that story. Suddenly, the worldview I had left North America with shattered. Yemen was a very wealthy nation, but little of that wealth had managed to trickle down to the people. As foreign corporations pumped the wealth of their nation onto tankers, it was obvious that many of the local citizens could barely feed themselves.

I could no longer view these poor, impoverished people as a threat to anyone. I began to wonder how many other nations that we'd seen on the news over the years had been impacted in the same way.

The question then shifted. I no longer wondered *if* we, in North America, were being deceived. That was now a given. Now, I wanted to know *why*.

A few days later, Dave returned to take over the crew and I was on my way home. The past few weeks had provided me with an interesting but confusing education, and I thought a lot about what I had learned on my flight back to Canada. Putting together the pieces of the puzzle was an interesting challenge. I thought about Perkins and the forces of good conscience that had led him away from his involvement in US foreign policy and prompted him to tell the world his truth about the system—a system which had effectively stolen much of the wealth of poorer nations all over the world. I thought about Yemen and wondered how the people there could be mired in such insidious poverty while living in such an incredibly oil rich nation. Where was their wealth going?

A couple of days later, I was home, standing in my kitchen with the television tuned to one of the major news channels. Something had changed: as I watched, I could no longer buy what they were selling. I picked up the remote and shut it off. I knew in my heart that there was a lot of truth out there that we weren't being told.

Little did I know that I had merely scratched the surface.

My phone rang later that day, and a friend explained that he and his wife were on their way to Toronto to attend a major international convention for people in recovery. I'd heard of these events, and my interest was piqued. It had been seven weeks since I had spent some quality time with the beautiful people who had loved me back to health, and this sounded like a perfect opportunity to reconnect.

The next day, I found myself on a Toronto-bound flight.

Toronto was a sight to behold. For the next three days, somewhere around fifty thousand recovering alcoholics and addicts took up residence in the downtown core. This was no typical convention: it was a comical, uplifting, spiritual extravaganza. As I walked down the street, I passed empty bars, where the staff had congregated on the sidewalk in front of their empty establishments. One bartender smiled and said, "We're not making any money, but we're sure meeting a lot of nice people." The local constabulary had relinquished their policing duties and were now acting as uniformed tour guides. They were laughing and joking with participants, and I'm sure they didn't make a single arrest that day.

At one point, I stood and surveyed the crowd as throngs of smiling, happy people from all over the world took over the Rogers

Centre, the home of the Toronto Blue Jays. I stared at them in awe. There were people here representing seventy-seven different nations. Every religion, ethnicity, skin colour, level of wealth and poverty—the entire *world*—was represented, and there was nothing but smiling, happy, contented people who were running on love and kindness. As I stood out in centre field soaking in the joy on display, I began to wonder if drinking had taken these people to the same depths it had taken me to. I wondered if their lives had been as turbulent as mine. I considered the millions of others from around the world whose lives, and whose loved ones' lives, had also been positively impacted by the design for living offered by recovery.

All of this—the program of recovery and the love and support—was freely given. There were no dues or fees and no financial strings of any kind attached. Through this freely given design for living, my sanity had become directly proportional to my willingness to step out of my own ego and be of service to others. The miracle of recovery rested on a very simple premise: by coming together to share our individual experience, strength, and hope, our lives had been transformed. The evidence to support this fact surrounded me and couldn't be argued with. One day at a time, love had not only saved me, but had also given me a life I had never dreamed was possible. And by the looks of this crowd, I wasn't alone.

My imagination then began to work overtime. I tried to grasp what would transpire if suddenly, truckloads of alcohol were to appear; what would ensue if we all slipped back into our egos and started drinking again. I smiled. It was almost comical to think that the beautiful experience currently playing out inside the Rogers Centre would quickly transform into anarchy, complete with SWAT teams, ambulances, fire engines, and paramedics.

I thought back to the insanity which, years before, had brought me to the edge of the abyss. It was a far cry from how I was living now. I had been desperate, alone, and suicidal. Here, in the now, things were very, very different.

The peace and the love that encapsulated that weekend in Toronto is something I hope I never forget. That day, standing in centre field surrounded by fifty thousand recovering alcoholics who were happy, joyous, and free, I contemplated the powerful example offered by those in recovery. I began to wonder if the people of the world could create a global community and learn to live in peace through a similar process.

I left Toronto at the end of that weekend with one predominant thought about the world we live in: millions of chronic alcoholics had been relieved of their insanity, starting with the simple understanding that they could no longer continue living as they had. Driven by desperation, they had chosen to embrace a simple, teachable spiritual design for living, and the results of that process were undeniable: these social outcasts had been transformed into the kindest, most peaceful people you'd ever care to meet. What had begun with two men supporting one another in 1935 had blossomed into millions sharing their experience, strength, and hope with each other—and every single one of them had begun their individual journey by clearly recognising that they could no longer continue as they had.

All of this led to one very significant question: if a bunch of drunks were capable of a transformation of this magnitude, why weren't we all?

The thought scratched at my soul. This perspective was like a new pair of glasses. I began to seriously consider whether the spiritual principles I had learned in recovery could resolve the problems I'd encountered as I'd travelled throughout our world.

By the time I returned to the Middle East, I had reached a point where I really wanted to know why things were the way they were. Recovery had taught me that change requires honesty, because without honesty, I would only be fooling myself — so, what, exactly, was true? Obviously, there must be something in it for someone, or there wouldn't be massive defence budgets allocated to financing wars. I struggled to accept the idea that entire nations had been and continue to be hoodwinked into supporting the killing of millions of people because of nothing more than the greed and a desire for power of a few. But that was exactly the pattern John Perkins had described in his book *Confessions of an Economic Hit Man*, and I was now witnessing living proof of Perkins' thesis.

A few weeks after the Toronto convention, I returned to Yemen believing that change on a large scale was not only possible, but also that I was a small but fundamental part of it. However, I wasn't delusional enough to think that the corporate and political leadership who profited from the wars and global insanity they created would suddenly wake up and see the errors of their ways.

After all, if the deaths of millions of innocent civilians hadn't been a sufficient deterrent, what would be?

For the next two years, I continued to work in Yemen. I loved my crew and most of the people I worked with were great. However, as luck would have it, the way my schedule worked out meant that I was consistently blessed with managing the two miserable alcoholic superintendents on the crew. Facing one was difficult; facing both at the same time proved to be a challenge.

The day eventually came when I witnessed one of them, who was suffering from a nasty hangover, explode in a vicious verbal attack toward one of the men, who was in the process of going home to his family after completing his one hundred and eightieth consecutive day of work (yes, one hundred and eighty days *in a row*).

I couldn't get that event out of my head during my subsequent days off. In the aftermath of that episode, when it came time for me to return to Yemen, I just couldn't get back on the plane.

"There is no such thing as coincidences. Nothing happens by mistake in this world," my good friend Norma often says. "Everything is designed to teach us, and it is up to us: we can either learn the lesson and move on or stay stuck in our own shit." Norma was packed full of love and wisdom, and nothing was sugarcoated when she spoke from her heart. So when my phone rang out of the blue a short time later (again) and the nice lady on the other end asked me if I wanted to go work in Libya for a North American drilling company, the little voice inside whispered an affirmative response.

I started packing.

Over the next few years, that process would repeat itself on numerous occasions, with my work taking me to Kuwait, Iraq, Romania, and Colombia.

For the record, I was never crazy about the work. Most of the management people I worked for were white men from North America, and while I met many wonderful people during my travels, I occasionally met a few with hateful, racist attitudes. There was one instance where I discovered I'd been hired to replace a man – a person of colour – who was exceptional at his job, and when I asked the manager why they were letting him go, the response I received was, "If it ain't white, it ain't right."

I immediately called Human Resources, explained the situation, and asked if they could find a job elsewhere for the man, adding, "While you're looking for him, look for me, too. I will not work for these people."

On a much brighter side, most of the local people I worked with in Libya, Iraq, Romania, and Colombia were second to none. Regardless of where I went, the honesty and respect of the local people I encountered consistently contradicted the cultural identity depicted by the mainstream media in North America. As my understanding of the real agenda became clearer, I could no longer see these people as "the enemy". I've subsequently come to believe that it's difficult to maintain huge defence budgets to wage war on nice people, so the story we're told demands the alternative.

Then came Afghanistan, where I travelled to investigate a

partnership opportunity in a contracting firm. I'd had numerous second thoughts about this trip, and my mother was very concerned for my safety. I attempted to calm her by explaining that many of the fears I'd had about past trips had consistently been unmerited, but that, of course, did little to ease her anxiety.

I arrived in Kabul with a reservation at a hotel with significant security, complete with Jersey barriers, razor wire, and heavily armed guards. On my second night there, I had dinner with a retired British army officer, who was working in Kabul as a contractor. At one point, Andy said, "Get up in the morning, walk out past security, and go for a stroll around town."

I laughed, thinking he was joking, and sarcastically replied, "Sure, I'll get right on that."

"I'm serious," he insisted. "This city is safer than Washington D.C. When something blows up here, everybody knows well in advance."

The next morning, I thought my heart was coming out of my chest as I walked out of the hotel and past security. The guards merely nodded as I continued down the street. I don't think I made it two blocks before I was apprehended by a seven-year-old girl and her nine-year-old brother. The boy struck me as having some developmental issues, but that little girl had great command of all her faculties, and those two kids took me all over that part of Kabul.

That day would become one of the greatest memories of my life. At the end of it, they beamed when I gave them twenty dollars. In hindsight, I wish I had given them much more.

After that, I continued to struggle with the thought that all too often, these are the people who suffer the most in the wars that are waged for profit.

My Afghan business venture never materialised. We just couldn't reach an agreement on several issues — a fact which delighted my mother. While the trip may not have been productive from a business perspective, the people I met and the lessons I learned made the venture worthwhile.

It would also become clear that my personal transformation was only just beginning.

4

A Life of Love

ONCE UPON A TIME, I made a conscious decision to open my heart to the Power of the Universe and to learn from others in recovery. What I have come to believe, based on these experiences in my life, is that if we listen — truly listen — to the whisper of our own souls, we come to intuitively know what the right thing to do is — or, at the very least, we come to know what the wrong thing to do is.

I have had many experiences which could only be described as miraculous since I made a commitment to live my life guided by spiritual principles. My introduction to plant medicine is high on that list.

In April of 2018, I was on the west coast of Nicaragua with my good friend Carlos. I'd had a dream of building an international spiritual healing centre for young people struggling with drug and alcohol abuse, and Carlos, being a great friend and one of the most knowledgeable real estate people I'd ever met, was helping me find a location.

While on the Pacific Coast, I received an email from a friend in recovery with a link to a YouTube video called *Mrs. Moon's Medicine*. Because I didn't have a strong enough phone signal in that remote part of Nicaragua, I was unable to view the video at that time, so I tucked it away in my memory bank with the intention of watching it when we returned to the city.

A couple of days later, we left that beautiful part of the world and began making our way back to Managua, where I was scheduled to catch a flight home to Canada. At that point in time, Nicaragua was arguably the most peaceful country in central America, but along the way, we began to see evidence of civil unrest, and we were fortunate to even get in and out of Granada. Crowds had gathered and were blocking many of the streets. From Granada through Masaya and onto Managua, we were forced to detour around several roadblocks and protests, though Carlos still managed to get me to the airport with time to spare.

What followed was a long, nervous wait at the airport, and as the violence on the streets escalated, United Airlines ultimately cancelled my flight. While the airline worked to resolve the flight issues, ten people died that night on the sad, angry streets of Managua.

The next day, United managed to get me as far as Houston, and at 7:30AM the following morning (long after I had originally been scheduled to be at home in Canada), I found myself sitting at Gate

C45 in the Houston airport. It was then that I remembered the *Mrs. Moon's Medicine* video my friend had sent me. We were thirty minutes away from boarding, and I thought I could just nicely squeeze it in before we departed.

Mrs. Moon's Medicine is a true story about a man named Gerry Powell who, despite facing numerous problems as a youth, managed to become a financially successful businessman. However, by his own admission and despite his financial successes, Gerry developed a serious drug and alcohol problem. As the insanity and wreckage piled up in Gerry's life, he attempted to resolve his substance abuse problems through traditional recovery programs, but those endeavours only led to limited success. Then, during a drug-and-alcohol-induced trip to the Philippines and in what appeared to be a final act of desperation, a series of bizarre "coincidences" unfolded, and Gerry found himself back across the Pacific in Costa Rica. There, he was introduced to Moughenda, a shaman from Gabon.

Now, you may think what comes up next is extreme, but desperate times often call for desperate measures, and Gerry was sure desperate.

Under the guidance of Moughenda, Gerry consumed iboga, a powerful hallucinogenic plant medicine grown primarily in Africa. What followed can best be described as a profound spiritual experience, in which Gerry was taken first to the moon and then back to his childhood. There, he was clearly shown that the root cause of his insanity, buried deep within his subconscious mind, was childhood sexual abuse. "Mrs. Moon" then provided Gerry with the opportunity to heal by giving him a new heart. That, and subsequent plant medicine experiences, led Gerry to create Rythmia, a medically licenced facility where others would be given the opportunity to experience the healing properties of ayahuasca, a similar plant medicine common to the Indigenous tribes of the Amazon region.

Throughout the video, I strongly identified with the insanity in Gerry's life, and I became increasingly more curious about the spiritual and healing benefits offered by ayahuasca.

What happened next completely blew my mind.

Just as the video ended, we were called to board our flight at Gate C45. I put my phone away, grabbed my gear, and got in line just as the public address system made another announcement: "Would Mr. Gerry Powell please report to Gate C44?"

I couldn't believe what I'd just heard. I wanted to run next door to see for myself, but because it was a full flight, I needed to board before all the overhead compartment space was gone, and I didn't want to lose my place in line.

That "coincidence" stayed with me.

By that point in my recovery journey, being sober had given me the opportunity to heal many of the underlying issues in my life, but I continued to suffer from bouts of depression and a decades-old feeling, like a small pebble in my shoe, that something else wasn't quite right. In therapy, I regularly discussed the details of my sister's death, but there was something deeper scratching at my memory. With the help of a therapist, I'd been taken back through the events of my life, but no amount of reflection seemed to resolve the issue, and I began to wonder if I was simply wasting time and money. There was something gnawing at me, and I just couldn't seem to get past it. Whatever it was, it seemed to play a role in my depression.

A few weeks after returning home from Nicaragua and the events in Houston, Billy, my longtime dear friend in recovery who had played such a huge role in loving me back to health, died of cancer. My life in sobriety sunk to a new low.

The thought of going to Rythmia was now frequently on my mind. My research into ayahuasca and other plant medicines uncovered some positive information regarding their success in treating addiction, depression, PTSD, and an assortment of other maladies. Yes, a few negative events related to plant medicines had also been reported, but those were rare. My research also revealed that the individuals involved in these events had a history of either mental illness or chronic drug use. I was comforted by the fact that Rythmia was a licenced medical facility and that the medical history of the patrons was scrutinised during the booking process. Plus, the intake information clearly stated which medications, prescribed or otherwise, were not to be mixed with ayahuasca.

As I considered the possibilities offered by ayahuasca, I recognised that my greatest concern was not my personal wellbeing, but what my friends in the recovery community would think about me indulging in mind-altering substances after being clean and sober for years. Despite the widely accepted use of massive amounts of pharmaceuticals in our society, I thought the consumption of ayahuasca may be viewed as hypocritical by my peers. After all, much of the focus within the recovery community was on avoiding such things.

Then again, these were the same people who had taught me the spiritual axiom that "there is no such thing as a coincidence" and "everything happens for a reason". I considered the bizarre events at the Houston airport and the many lessons I had learned during my global travels. All of these had helped me grow and develop in many aspects of my life. I had been taught to trust my intuition, and I now felt as if I was being guided in the direction of Rythmia and the plant medicine experience.

Shortly after Billy's death, the news of Anthony Bourdain's suicide hit me hard and pushed me even deeper into my depression. Perhaps there was something more here I needed to learn. Besides, why would I *not* take advantage of every available opportunity to heal?

I picked up the phone and called Rythmia.

I arrived at Rythmia with concern and scepticism. I wondered whether this was just a major waste of time and money.

It was a Sunday. My first ayahuasca ceremony would not take place until the following Monday evening. Many of the week's eighty or so guests had already arrived, and we were encouraged to participate in a "breathwork" exercise that was scheduled for later that afternoon. This exercise was being facilitated by Christian Minson, a gentleman who had spent much of his life as a monk. He informed us that through the breathwork practice he was about to introduce us to, people were frequently able to process the trauma created by repressed past emotions.

On a personal level, I wasn't exactly sure what any of that meant, and I smiled to myself disbelievingly. Still, I concluded that I had been breathing for much of my life and it hadn't hurt me thus far, so I went along with it.

We were instructed to lay back, relax, and breathe rapidly into our lungs and bellies. It took a bit to coordinate the process, and Christian was assisted by several staff members who mingled with the crowd, offering support and suggestions on technique. All the while, the beat of jungle drums played loudly on the sound system.

It was a simple process, but it was also hard work, and after thirty minutes or so, I began to get tired and wonder what the point of it all was. By the time another ten minutes had gone by, I started to feel frustrated, and I threw in the towel. The entire exercise felt pointless.

A few seconds later, as I lay there surrounded by strangers, one of the most bizarre experiences of my life took place. Suddenly, I was transported back to June 24, 1969. I sat in the back seat of the family car with my arms wrapped around my mother as both of our hearts broke. My father, who was in the front seat, turned to look at me and said, "Why did you build the raft?"

The experience was not a passing thought. It was visceral and felt every bit as real as it had the day my sister had drowned.

The dam burst. The heartache, pain, and guilt that had been buried deep down inside of me for over fifty years erupted and flowed freely. I wept and clung to Stacey, one of the staff members who had graciously filled in as my surrogate mother. I'm not sure how long I clung to her and wept, but by the time it was over, the emotional burden I had carried for much of my life was, miraculously, gone.

As I returned to the present moment, Stacey smiled and slowly released me. I wiped away the tears and looked around. A few of those closest to me were staring, unsure of what had just transpired. All I knew for sure was that something deep inside of me had been released, and that I was much better off for it. The depression I'd arrived with had vanished, and I felt a freedom I had never known before.

The world looked very different the following morning. I just couldn't seem to wipe the smile off my face. I paused for a few minutes to look back at the spiritual transformation which had begun years earlier, starting with the simple realisation that I could no longer continue as I had. I was grateful to the Group Of Drunks I had met in recovery who had introduced me to the simple design for living that had allowed me to escape the insanity of my own ego. I was also grateful for the many experiences I'd had so far to see, firsthand, so much of the world. I held dear the lessons I had learned from those who had crossed my path and had even become grateful for the difficulties in my life that had motivated me to grow and learn. I was grateful for the knowledge that I would always have a choice in how I responded to the challenges that life put in my path. I was especially grateful for the unexpected gift provided by my breathwork experience. This had allowed me to experience and release the emotional pain of my sister's death, which had been buried deep within my subconscious mind for decades. Stepping into the light didn't do anything for me until I acknowledged the darkness.

I had come here for the miracle offered by ayahuasca, and even though I hadn't yet had that experience, I was already grateful beyond all measure for the gifts I'd received by coming to Rythmia.

Later that morning, we attended the group orientation, where Gerry described what we might expect during our first experience with ayahuasca. Based on the knowledge of the Indigenous people of the Amazon (who had been working with ayahuasca for thousands of years) and supported by the feedback from the thousands of people who had already participated in the Rythmia experience, Gerry briefed us on the various possibilities that may unfold during an ayahuasca ceremony.

Gerry explained that we are born with a soul—a spirit—that is the true essence of who we really are. At birth, our soul knows only love—nothing of hate or violence—but as our intellect develops in early childhood, we arrive at an understanding of how we *think* the world works and the nature of our relationship with it. We make these judgements based on our upbringing and the society we are born into. We also develop an ego—a persona we create based on how we want the world to see us. We come to rely more and more upon the power of our mind, and we slowly distance ourselves from our true, authentic nature and the whisper of our own soul.

Depending on familial and cultural influences, many of us, without really knowing it, maintain a sense of balance in our lives between our egos and our souls. We somehow intuitively know deep down inside what acceptable behaviour is and what it isn't.

However, for those who have been raised in environments heavily dominated by the ego or who have experienced trauma (especially in early childhood), the ego steps to the forefront and assumes a much greater level of control of our lives. The sense of balance, empathy, and loving kindness that would otherwise have been rooted in our souls is lost as the ego quietly slips into the driver's seat and dominates every facet of our lives—and, once in control, the ego will go to any lengths to defend this position of power.

In my own case, I felt this assertion to have some merit. There was no other reasonable explanation for the insanity in my life. What else could possibly motivate an individual to act as I had? After hearing Gerry's story and the stories of hundreds of others in recovery, this pattern seemed too consistent to deny. I had, after years of recovery, come to believe that the insanity which had played such a devastating role in my life had been a direct result of my ego. As far as I could see, the only thing that had granted me a shred of sanity had come courtesy of a spiritual experience—an experience which had been in the making since my final visit to the detox centre so many years before.

After years of trudging the spiritual path, I was very aware that I was neither unique nor alone. I'd heard the stories of many others who had shared similar experiences. (That said, all I have is my own story, and I am not an authority on the workings of the human mind.) Gerry's rudimentary explanation was consistent with much of what I had learned during my years in recovery. As a father, I knew that my children, despite having so much in common, had been very different people from the moment they were born. I had also become acutely aware of the separation between my intellect and my own soul; of the distinct differences between the rants of my ego and the whispers of the little voice inside.

Looking back years later, I still have no other plausible explanation for my own insanity. My ego, left unchecked and given free rein, had all but killed me. The spiritual and soulful development I'd come to enjoy had been a direct result of my desperate willingness to listen and learn from the experience of others, while learning to trust the whisper of the little voice deep down inside.

Gerry explained that the goal of the ceremonies that would take place over the course of the next four nights was to heal. The medicine, we were told, was extremely intelligent and would do for us what was most necessary to help us heal. For most of us, that would take the form of a spiritual experience which would heal our hearts and reunite us with our own souls — the true, authentic self which our ego had pushed aside as it usurped control of our lives.

There are thousands of years of history supporting the use of this medicine by the tribes in the Amazon region, so much so that these ceremonies have developed their own folklore and language. Accordingly, I began to pick up on frequent references to Mother Ayahuasca and the Divine Mother. My interpretation of this landed somewhere between Mother Nature, the Soul of the Universe, and the Creator. I related it all to the spiritual stories I had learned from the many Indigenous people I'd had the pleasure of sharing my time in recovery with over the years. There was a natural wisdom and sensibility to their knowledge that I found to be lacking in so many of western culture's religions.

For the next four nights, the eighty or so participants gathered in a big room, where we each had our own mattress. As the ceremony began, we formed two lines — one for men and one for women — and were served the worst tasting stuff I have ever consumed (and I say that having drunk some horrendous stuff in my past). We then returned to our respective mattresses. All we could do was wait for the medicine to do what it did and trust it to take us where we needed to go.

To explain in detail what transpired that week, and in the other plant medicine retreats I later attended in Costa Rica, Colombia, and Peru, would take volumes. To say I merged back with my soul would be an understatement. Even for a guy who had lived much of his life immersed in an altered state, there was no benchmark for what the ayahuasca experience offered. The problem you, the reader, may encounter when trying to understand this lies in the limits of your own imagination. It really is difficult to put into words what the plant medicine experience is like. Had I not had the benefit of numerous detailed discussions with other participants (many of whom had had prior experience with ayahuasca), I may not have believed what I went through myself. The best explanation I can provide is that the medicine took me deep into myself. Everything I experienced was deeply personal to me. I never simply observed a scenario that wasn't personal and soulful.

I basically had spiritual surgery where real physical ailments of mine were addressed in several different ways. On several occasions, I returned to the comfort of my own mother's womb and experienced being reborn. There was also a sense of humour about it all: a nurse who actually delivered babies at her job and was occupying the mattress next to me assisted my rebirth on one particular night not once, but twice.

Along with these spiritual rebirths, I also experienced several spiritual deaths. On one occasion, I was lying in a grave watching people shovel dirt on top of me. I felt no fear as I sank lower and lower. I ultimately arrived at a peaceful place, where I was reunited with my father, my little sister, my good friend Billy, and several other friends who had passed away.

It is said the medicine always works in your best interests but will never give you more than you can handle. That said, once ingested, there is no stopping the experience, and any attempt to avoid what the medicine is trying to teach you only adds another level of anxiety to the process. The best advice I received about managing the more difficult moments was to simply kick back, embrace the experience, and watch the movie that unfolds. I also found it beneficial to remind myself that the best lessons often come from the most difficult times. Indeed, there were events from my past—some rooted deep in my subconscious and buried under years of drinking—that I needed to clearly see, experience, and understand in order to heal. For example, it was painful but necessary for me to see, in graphic detail, what it had been like for my ex-wife and children to live with me when my alcoholism had been out of control.

The most beautiful nights often followed the difficult ones, and I have yet to leave a retreat without a profound sense of gratitude for what the medicine taught me.

There is one story I feel obligated to share. It's not only amusing, but also relevant to the subject matter:

During one of the ceremonies, Sarah, one of the beautiful souls at Rythmia, poured me a second serving of ayahuasca. As she offered it to me, a man's voice spoke firmly and very clearly from deep within me: "If you drink this, you will die." Nothing like this had ever happened to me before, and it caught me off guard. Somewhat frightened, I handed the medicine back to Sarah. I told her what had happened, and she suggested I leave it and go back to my mattress, which I did. Hearing voices is common during ceremonies, but still, I'm not sure how long I sat processing the scenario. At some point, I began to question where, exactly, that voice had come from. Was it my soul, or was it my ego?

I went back to Sarah, who had initially suggested I return to my mattress and meditate. Once I told her that I actually wanted another drink, she broke into a smile and said, "The medicine gives life. It doesn't take life." She poured me a small drink and I returned to my mattress.

As the medicine worked its magic, a strange, tall, slim man with a ghostly grey face, dressed in a big black hat and a long black trench coat, appeared at the foot of my mattress. He didn't acknowledge me. Getting down on one knee, he placed a small white box on the floor and, producing a small shovel, began digging a hole. I watched him dig. When he seemed satisfied with the hole, he suddenly looked at me, stretched out his hand, and said, "Give me your ego." Even under the influence of the medicine,

I thought, *This is nuts.* Still, I reached out with a closed fist and dropped my "ego" into his open hand. He opened the little white box, placed my ego into it, and closed the lid. He then put the box in the hole, covered it up, stood, and walked away.

I was blown away by this bizarre series of events and sat back when it was over, trying to make sense of it.

It had taken some courage to have that second drink, but I had come to trust the spiritual process that had led me to this place and Mother Ayahuasca. *If you drink this, you will die.* It occurred to me that what I had just witnessed had been the death of my ego. Of course, I still have an ego, but what I experienced was the clear distinction between my ego and my soul, and a reminder of the fact that I have a choice in which one I listen to.

There were a few reoccurring experiences which came up nearly every night, and because of their frequency, I began to pay closer attention to them. One which came to me every night during my second trip to Rythmia was a vision of a massive billboard along Interstate 405, close to LAX in Los Angeles. The billboard had a solid pink background and displayed only four words in white: *You Can't Stop Love.* At the end of the last night, as I lay on my mattress slowly coming out of the experience, I asked Mother Ayahuasca if there was "anything else". A second passed and a brilliant, beautiful light appeared and wrapped itself around me. An angel's voice whispered in my ear, "Johnny, you are nothing but love, and you can't stop love."

If I could bottle how I felt at that moment, I'd put every drug dealer and distillery out of business forever. But it didn't stop there.

A few hours later, when I went in for lunch, I ran into Raksha, a beautiful soul from London. She looked at me and said, "I have a message for you. The Mother came to me last night and said, 'Tell John he's beautiful and that I love him.'" Upon hearing her words, I cracked, and tears ran down my cheeks. What an incredible life I was living.

Addiction is a spiritual malady, and many of the people I have met at plant medicine retreats have either been in recovery themselves or been healers or therapists working in the field of addiction. The latter group attended retreats to gain firsthand experience of the medicine so they could better guide their clients through the healing process. Today, ibogaine and ayahuasca, despite being illegal in the USA, have been used by thousands of people around the world for the treatment of a variety of maladies, including opiate addiction, alcoholism, depression, and posttraumatic stress disorder (PTSD).

For years, I had fought everyone and everything to get what I thought I wanted, but it was only when I surrendered and stopped fighting that I was able to gratefully accept the gifts the universe was trying to freely give me. Only then was I able to find any real happiness. The truth I had to accept was that I had no control over my ex-wife, the courts, past employers, or the world in general, so there was no point in fighting with them, nor was getting drunk and being angry going to bring my sister back. There were many thoughts fueling my insanity that I had to either accept or let go of, and it was virtually impossible for me to accomplish either if I was drunk.

The little voice deep inside me that initially tried to nudge me in the right direction during my drinking days has become an even greater source of peace in my life as I've learned to trust it. When I become still and search inside for the answers, I usually discover what the right thing to do is. If not, I do, at the very least, get a very good idea of what the wrong thing to do is. Slowly, as the years have passed, the negative actions and reactions rooted in my ego have been revealed, unlearned, and replaced by a much kinder process.

Today, I can honestly say that becoming an alcoholic has been one of the greatest gifts of my life. Had my insanity not driven me to the point where I was desperate enough to allow love to save my sorry ass, you would have found me glued to the front end of a Mack truck, or worse. Instead, love intervened, and I came to see that I had a choice. I could choose love and do the right thing rather than buying into the fear, the selfishness, and the need to control others. As a result of one simple decision, the entire trajectory of my life changed. My new life doesn't resemble my old one in the slightest.

I've always found it amusing when "normal" people openly express their remorse when I tell them I don't drink. "Oh, I'm sorry," they often say, as if I've developed a terminal illness and lost the will to live. In fact, I have *found* the will to live, and my life in recovery is much more interesting, not to mention more important, than my life on a barstool ever was. Not only have I become the world's greatest great-grandfather, but I've also been given the opportunity to travel the world and meet some extraordinary people along the way.

I've always appreciated the sarcasm in my friend Doug's thoughts when he frequently tells us, "Had I only known what I know today when I was younger, I would have drunk more sooner just to get to recovery earlier."

Today, thirty years into this experiment, I've had numerous experiences that could only be described as miraculous, and I've heard hundreds of similar stories from the beautiful souls I've met in recovery rooms from all over the world.

Again, I must ask, if a bunch of drunks can be relieved of their insanity and become the kindest, most peaceful people on the planet, why can't we all?

5

Uncle Sam's Bender

OVER THE YEARS FOLLOWING MY initial trip to Yemen and my realisation that the story we were being told was nothing more than that—a story—I began to pay close attention to the reality of life as I travelled through Libya, Kuwait, Iraq, and Afghanistan.

I wanted to be wrong. I wanted, more than anything else, to find a shred of evidence which supported the military's massive investment into the deaths of millions and the destruction of entire civilisations.

If that evidence existed, it never crossed my path.

Throughout these years, I read volumes written by those who are internationally recognised for their knowledge or direct involvement in the creation and implementation of the global policies that have shaped our world. I realise that I have only scratched the surface here, but my list includes Noam Chomsky, Seymour Hersh, Chris Hedges, Megan Stack, John Stockwell, Joel Andreas, S. Brian Willson, and, of course, John Perkins. It has also become obvious that these individuals, despite being Americans and globally recognised experts in their fields, are rarely, if ever, interviewed by the mainstream media in North America. Clamor regarding censorship, book bans, and the teaching of the "correct" view of history is currently raging, and, indeed, I am convinced that the control of information and the indoctrination of the masses has been well underway for decades now. Please feel free to suggest that this is simply another "conspiracy theory", but the truth is that rarely has a member of Veterans for Peace, or Noam Chomsky (who's had a hand in the publication of more than a hundred books regarding US foreign policy), appeared on CNN. Ted Nugent, however — the rockstar who authored such thoughtful overtures as *Wango Tango* — frequently appeared on CNN in support of America's foreign policy agenda.

Does anyone else wonder why?

I've also read numerous government and agency documents, many of which were once classified, including The Church Report, which was the result of a congressional investigation into the actions of the various intelligence organisations in America. I've watched documentaries on this topic, and *The War You Don't See* by John Pilger is a disturbing account of how the media functions in step with the US military to inform, or perhaps misinform, the public regarding the wars being fought.

I view the past seventy-five years of corporate and political leadership in our world in much the same way that I would look at a group of selfish, self-centred, chronic drunks who are attempting to convince themselves and everyone else that they "have everything all figured out" while the wreckage piles up in their wake.

The thought precedes the action, so the problem wasn't the war, or the booze, or the drugs. By now, I was convinced the real problem was an addiction — a need for *more* that could never be satisfied — which was rooted in the mind and fueled by the insanity of the ego.

I also believed that addiction, when left untreated, leads to insanity, destroying everything in its path before ultimately killing the host. In my personal life, regardless of my attempts to either ignore or rationalise it, addiction led me to one irrefutable conclusion: I had been insane, and if I expected to survive, I could no longer continue to live as I had. If anything was ever going to change, it was mandatory that I get honest and stop deluding myself.

There were some hard lessons learned during my time in the Middle East, and it no longer mattered how I arranged the pieces of the puzzle. The picture was clear and consistent: most, if not all, the wars being fought had been created and forced upon the people of this world by rich men who wanted *more*. Millions had died in these wars — wars which were typically paid for with the people's tax dollars, even as entire populations were deprived of decent education and healthcare — and while the costs of these wars were the taxpayer's responsibility, the spoils of them were not. These were only being distributed among the ranks of the corporate and political elite of our nations. The people got the bill while the "already wealthy beyond all measure" got the loot. None of this was complicated.

I began to wonder, how much longer could we continue as we had before our global leadership, running on ego and drunk on greed and power, destroyed all of us, along with the host, Mother Earth?

My friends in recovery had suggested I read a few spiritual books, and there was no debate: apparently, my mind had been pried open enough by this point that I could seriously consider ideas I would have shunned in the past. I was fascinated by Neale Donald Walsch's series *Conversations with God*, in which he documents a personal dialogue he has with the "God" of *his understanding*. Throughout his work, Walsch reveals a great deal of insight into how the universe functions. It is logical, thoughtful, and sensible. His personal, non-religious perspective led me to the realisation that the world is, indeed, perfect—well, at least, it *was*, until man, armed with his "free will", decided to run the show and start playing God.

Eckhart Tolle was another spiritual philosopher that made a great deal of sense to me. While reading his book *A New Earth*, I read the following quote and literally burst out laughing:

> Fear, greed, and the desire for power are the psychological motivating forces not only behind warfare and violence between nations, tribes, religions,

and ideologies, but also the cause of incessant conflict in personal relationships. They bring about a distortion in your perception of other people and yourself. Through them, you misinterpret every situation, leading to misguided action designed to rid you of fear and satisfy your need for more, a bottomless hole that can never be filled.

It is important to realize, however, that fear, greed, and the desire for power are not the dysfunction that we are speaking of, but are themselves created by the dysfunction, which is a deep-seated collective delusion that lies within the mind of every human being. A number of spiritual teachings tell us to let go of fear and desire. But those spiritual practices are usually unsuccessful. They haven't gone to the root of the dysfunction. Fear, greed, and the desire for power are not the ultimate causal factors. Trying to become a good or better human being sounds like a commendable and high-minded thing to do, yet it is an endeavor you cannot ultimately succeed in unless there is a shift in consciousness. This is because it is still part of the same dysfunction, a more subtle and rarified form of self-enhancement, of desire for more and a strengthening of one's conceptual identity, one's self-image. You do not become good by trying to be good, but by finding the goodness that is already within you, and allowing that goodness to emerge. But it can only emerge if something fundamental changes in your state of consciousness.

The history of Communism, originally inspired by noble ideals, clearly illustrates what happens when people attempt to change external reality — create a new earth — without any prior change in their inner reality, their state of consciousness. They make plans without taking into account the blueprint for dysfunction that every human being carries within: the ego.[2]

I read this passage again and again. Was this another "coincidence"?

What I found so incredibly amusing in Tolle's words was that he had just described addiction. His words had taken me back to that meeting so very early in my recovery in which I had been taught that fear, selfishness, and the need to control were the psychological motivating forces, rooted in the ego of alcoholics, that had taken us to drink. I saw no difference between "fear, greed, and the desire for power" and "fear, selfishness, and the need for control". My ego, thought process, and belief system had been the root cause of my alcoholism, while the egos of others had led them to create wars, hoard wealth, foster racism, corrupt governments, destabilise nations, commit genocide, and so on.

Was it conceivable that the insanity of my ego, in which my addiction was rooted, was akin to the insanity of the egos who were responsible for creating the wars in our world? Motivated by fear,

---

2 Tolle, E. (2005): *A New Earth* (p.p. 12–13). New York: Penguin.

greed, and a desire for power, was our political and corporate leadership addicted to war? The thought precedes the action, so was it possible that all of mankind's insane maladies were a manifestation of the selfish, self-centred, never-satisfied, identifiable ego? If that was the case, was it possible that the same teachable spiritual solution designed to deflate the ego — the same solution that had delivered a shred of peace and sanity to the lives of millions of insane addicts and alcoholics — could also heal those addicted to the insanity of war? Of hate? Of racism? I think so. In fact, I believe that there is no other way. As Tolle points out, the ego (i.e., how we think) is the root cause of practically every single dilemma mankind faces, and the solution lies in a *fundamental change in our state of consciousness.* This *fundamental change* is exemplified by the millions who have already successfully made that transformation, courtesy of spiritual recovery programs.

We all have an ego. The creation of nuclear weapons, slavery, racism, genocide, political corruption, and the destruction of rainforests are all exemplified by man selfishly playing God. Whether it be war, booze, food, sex, gambling, or an unlimited desire to acquire more wealth and power, the *need for more* is the common denominator in all of man's addictions. One man would lose his job, family, and even his life to alcohol, while others would kill millions in wars for the global control of oil and drugs. Both men are insane; both men often rationalise their actions through stories concocted by their egos. Because both actions are repeated over and over with insane results, I ask you if both qualify as addictions. Are not both shining examples of the insanity that defines addiction?

The only thing in Tolle's thesis that I questioned was his comment regarding communism. It isn't that I disagreed — not at all — but if war was rooted in the ego, what could be said regarding *all* the wars created by America? What about the genocide perpetrated against the Native American communities and the slavery and racism which is deeply embedded in American society? It seemed that nothing was static and even the best intentions could be distorted and could fall prey to the desire for power, rooted in the ego.

Tolle's account was published in 2005, and since then, the world has undergone some serious growing pains. American corporations and the politicians who cater to them have lobbied hard for deregulation, which has led to even greater corporate control of our governments. Capitalism has become predatory. There is rarely even a discussion of peace; the world now resembles the "winner take all" ideology of the wild west, where might makes right. Corporations with tremendous political and economic influence have been declared to have the same rights as people by courts where judges are appointed by politicians who are heavily influenced by wealthy corporate elites.

The people, who are supposed to have the power in this grand experiment called democracy, are getting the bill, while the corporations, which now own and control the executive branches of our governments, are either getting massive tax cuts or aren't paying any taxes at all.

I ask, is this a soulful process? Or is this the work of the ego?

Have these corporations considered what is in the best interests of the people in this world, or are they selfishly motivated by fear, greed, and a desire for power?

Is it working? Is it sustainable? Is it making the world a better place?

I have come to believe that it is not only communism that is the work of the ego; any extremist political ideology is the work of the ego, including the current predatory form of capitalism (which also happens to be the driving force behind all our wars for profit). When we look at left wing versus right, I see Stalin and Mao on one end and Hitler on the other, but when I consider the results of their actions, they are all eerily similar: violent, oppressive, and murderous. Despite being at opposite ends of the political spectrum, isn't it obvious that their extreme actions are rooted in greed and a desire for power, and that they exemplify the insanity of the ego's need for more?

These issues may appear to be political or economic in nature, but the truth is, they form the *spiritual* dilemma which lies at the very root of all our problems. There must be something terribly dysfunctional within the soul of mankind when the need to control others is so blatant and violent. In our attempt to rationalise our insanity, we delude ourselves into believing that the problem is political or economic, or that it may require a military solution, when the truth is that it is a spiritual issue.

As we've already discussed, the ego strives to remain in a position of control. It loves being in charge, and nothing threatens it more than an honest and truthful evaluation. Its need to maintain its position of power and control is so strong that laws in our society are constructed to prevent such an evaluation from taking place. There are myriad examples of this in recent history. Two of the most recent are Julian Assange, who was imprisoned for exposing the truth regarding America's war crimes, and Edward Snowden, who is in exile for informing the American people that their own government has been spying on them.

Vital to any kind of transformation is the understanding that how we think and what we believe dictates how we act, and that if our thoughts are rooted in ego-induced fear, greed, and desire for power, chances are that the outcome isn't going to be pleasant, regardless of whether these actions take place within the home or on the international stage. The same kind of thinking that caused the problem can't solve the problem.

How can we, the global community, ever hope to evolve and live in a higher state of consciousness if we do not take into account *the blueprint for dysfunction that every human being carries within: the ego?*

Case in point: in 2018, shortly after the mass shooting at Stoneman Douglas High School in Parkland, Florida, I was travelling through Fort Worth, Texas. An old friend had once lived there and told me that Fort Worth was my kind of town, so I decided to spend some time looking around. As I was checking in, the hotel concierge informed me that the shuttle was about to take a group down to the Stockyards, the historical and main tourist area of the city, and there was room for me, if I wanted to go. A few minutes later, I found myself outside chatting with the driver. As the back of the shuttle filled with people, he suggested I hop in the front so we could continue our discussion. I told him that I was a

Canadian driving from Mexico to Canada. He said he was a schoolteacher who was moonlighting for a few extra dollars.

"A teacher?" I asked, instantly thinking of the recent shooting. "Are you packing?"

He grinned and said, "No, but I would if I could. They won't let us."

"No worries. Guns aren't the problem anyhow."

"If guns aren't the problem, what do you think is the problem?"

It took a split second for me to realise that engaging in this debate may not be the easiest way for me to make friends in Texas. Here I was, a peace-loving Canadian offering my perspective to Texans about their guns while, in the aftermath of another mass shooting, the Second Amendment debate was once again raging across the USA.

I glanced into the back of the shuttle to discover that everyone was staring at me, waiting for me to respond. "Ahh, you don't really want to hear what a Canadian thinks," I shrugged, feigning lightheartedness.

"But I do," he insisted. "If guns aren't the problem, what do you believe is?"

I had backed myself into a corner and could see no way out other than through speaking from the heart and honestly sharing what I had learned during my global travels. Throwing caution to the wind, I said, "The problem is how you think. If you can take a kid out of high school, give him an assault rifle, send him to the other side of the world, and teach him that we solve our problems by killing others, why would that same logic not be acceptable at home? The belief that violence is the solution is inherent in America's collective thought process. On the world stage, killing people is as American as apple pie, which is the reason why the USA leads the world in gun violence. The thought precedes the action, and if the thought process is violent, the outcome will be violent. If we can clearly see this, we might all want to ask ourselves if it's working. Is all this insanity making the world a better place?"

The driver looked at me and nodded. Nobody else said a word.

But let's examine a situation a little less close to home: have you ever wondered how a madman like Hitler was able to command such a great deal of support from the German people? It would have been a short war had he decided to take on the world all by himself, but he was somehow able to convince a significant portion of the German people to go to war on his behalf. What kind of *story* were the people told that would convince them to leave their families and their jobs as schoolteachers and plumbers to go to war and kill their neighbours? How could the German people have allowed this to happen? How could they be convinced to partake in the genocide that was taking place all around them?

I know I'm not the only one to ever ask those questions. In her book *Caste*, author Isabel Wilkerson examines Nazi Germany to gain a clearer understanding of racism in the United States. Her research led to interviews with German citizens who lived just outside the gates of concentration and extermination camps.

The ash rose from the crematorium into the air, carried
by karma and breeze, and settled onto the front steps

and geraniums beds of the townspeople living outside the gates of death at Sachsenhausen, north of Berlin. The ash coated the swing sets and paddling pools in the backyards of the townspeople.

There was no denying the slaughter and torment on the other side of the barbed wire. The fruit of evil fell upon villagers like snow dust. They were covered in evil, and some were good parents and capable spouses, and yet they did nothing to stop the evil, which had now grown too big for one person to stop, and thus no person was complicit, and yet everyone was complicit. It had grown bigger than them because they had allowed it to grow bigger than them, and now it was raining down onto their gingerbread cottages and their lives of pristine conformity.[3]

Individuals in leadership roles who function exclusively from the ego will ultimately create organisations and nations that reflect their egos' values. Their thoughts and actions will be motivated by fear, greed, and the desire for power—all so they can feed their insatiable need for *more*.

Hitler's Germany provides us with an excellent example of the national ego at work. The millions of lives lost due to Hitler's desire for power could have easily been saved, had the German public understood and recognised the insane ways of the ego and held their leadership to a higher standard. I will argue that we, the

---

[3] Wilkerson, I. (2020): *Caste* (p. 89). New York: Random House.

citizens in the west, have failed in much the same way — that is, in our responsibility to hold our governments accountable. In a democracy, the people are supposed to have the power, but corporations — especially those who profit from weapons, oil, and drugs — have garnered far greater power than was intended when the concept of democracy was created. Nationalism, not unlike that of Nazi Germany, has been fostered by those who live in the ego, and the hallmarks of fear, greed, and the desire for power are evident for all to see.

Many wear this nationalism with pride, and there is nothing wrong with loving your country. But is killing your neighbours to satisfy the need for *more* of those who are already wealthy beyond all measure creating a better world for your children? Does this nationalism and patriotism really accomplish anything positive? Or does it, in egoic fashion, simply blind us to the truth regarding our own collective action (or, more accurately, inaction)?

Following the attacks of September 11, nationalism hit an all-time high. "You are either with us or against us," George W. Bush stated on November 6, 2001, as the buildup for the invasion of Afghanistan took place. Now, years later, many have started to wonder whether the corporate agenda leading up to the Afghan invasion was centred on accruing proceeds from weapons sales and the control of the opium trade. After all, there is very little evidence to suggest that the Afghan people played even a small role in 9/11, yet citizens and taxpayers of the USA invested trillions of their tax dollars for the twenty years of war in Afghanistan — a war that the American people may never have supported, had they not been emotionally wounded by the attacks of 9/11.

Today, we have an opportunity to not just evaluate the destruction which occurred on 9/11, but to also conduct an honest appraisal of our response to those events. Accordingly, I ask you, was the invasion of Afghanistan, and later Iraq, beneficial in any way to anyone but the few who profited in billions?

My goal is not to convince you that I hold the "correct" view of history. You, of course, are allowed to believe whatever you wish. My only real goal is to invite you to question, with rigorous honesty, what *you* believe. If you subscribe to the theory that the people truly do hold the power in democracy, then it is incumbent on the people to know and demand the truth. Ask yourself, who benefits when an entire nation believes that holding itself accountable is no longer necessary? Have we, like an alcoholic in the throes of his addiction, become numb to the reality of our actions?

Hitler was obsessed with race, so the story conveyed to the German people was that the Aryan race was superior to all others. This story laid the groundwork for the deaths of six million Jews, among millions of others. "Repeat a lie often enough and it becomes the truth," is a quote attributed to Joseph Goebbels, Hitler's chief propagandist. I would venture a guess that almost everyone in recovery will smile and nod upon reading this. Prior to recovery, a drunk, running on ego, will say almost anything to get what he wants—yet give him some time in recovery, where his life actually depends on developing the honesty to face the truth of who and what he truly is, and he will undergo an amazing transformation and become one of the most trustworthy and reliable human beings you would ever wish to meet.

Today, the pendulum has swung back as Israel, under its Zionist leadership, indiscriminately bombs an unarmed Gaza, while those nations who profit in billions from the sale of weapons continue to support the slaughter.

What is wrong with us? What kind of people support this level of insanity? Can we continue as we have? Have you had enough yet?

We often hear the phrase "soul of a nation", but would the soul (which is where patience, tolerance, and love emanate from) tolerate the wars, the hate, the slavery, and the racism our nations perpetuate? After conducting a fearless and thorough moral inventory of itself, would the soul of a nation be pleased to discover that over fifty percent of its taxbase funds a military that's killed millions and that it has been at war for two hundred and twenty-seven years out of the past two hundred and forty-five? Would the soul be pleased to learn that our elected officials created these wars simply to facilitate the sale of weapons and the theft of resources? Would the soul be delighted with the widespread corruption prevalent within a political system where the wealthy few have purchased control of our democracies?

If this is acceptable and condoned by the general population, is the soul of the nation really at work? Or is this the work of the national ego?

I once heard it said that if there's one attribute capable of determining the financial success of a CEO, it is a complete lack of empathy. This is concerning. To live with no regard for the wellbeing of your fellow man is selfish and soulless and embodies the insanity of the ego — and to create wars merely for profit is the epitome of insanity. Yet it also makes logical sense when some of the basic tenets of capitalism are understood. Every business in the world strives to expand its market and increase market share, so how does one achieve that goal when they're in the business of killing people? When the business of war is funded by the people who pay the taxes, what kind of story will those who are addicted to the profits of war be telling their citizens to keep them complicit?

Once again, I ask you, can we continue as we have? Those in recovery were once forced to ask themselves that same question, and millions of them came to the realisation that they had a choice and went on to create brand-new lives, leaving behind those who were incapable of seeing that they, too, had a choice. In a similar fashion, there may always be those who choose to be motivated by the insanity of their ego and remain engaged in wars for profit, all too often taking innocent lives with them. On an ever-increasing basis, however, more and more of the world's people are recognising that we stand at a turning point and that our continuing as we have will culminate in our own destruction. By adopting a handful of spiritual principles, millions of people, one person at a time, have recognised the need for change and have been restored to sanity. The result has been a design for living which has brought peace, love, and kindness into the lives of people all over the world.

Have you ever been to the Palace of Versailles? Every year, throngs of tourists flock to Versailles to see its beauty. Upon arriving, it didn't take me long to understand why the lavish grounds and Versailles' two thousand rooms, complete with its solid silver chairs, became contributing factors to the French Revolution. As the people of France starved to death under the weight of heavy taxation, the opulence of Versailles signified the disparity between the people and the nobility, which had become increasingly corrupt.

France wasn't alone. Throughout the European feudal system, a relatively small group of wealthy aristocrats owned practically all the land, made up all the laws, held all the wealth and political control, and had the power to tax their vassals at will—and this system was failing throughout Europe. At the same time, on the other side of the Atlantic and following the American Revolution, democracy was taking root. When the opportunity to own land, be free, have a voice and a choice in shaping one's own future, and have equality and justice was beginning to blossom, millions of immigrants left the corrupt inequities of Europe to start a new life in the Americas.

How's that working out? Haven't we come full circle?

Today, the leadership in most, if not all, western nations claim that their policies embody freedom and democracy. Yet the truth we all know is that a handful of wealthy modern-day aristocrats own and control our world.

Ask yourself if our "democracies" are failing for the same reasons feudalism, and every other political system ever created, has failed. Aren't the concepts of equality, liberty, and justice nothing more than part of the *story* we've been told as the wealthy seek to satisfy their need for *more*?

Didn't Rome rot from within?

It's sobering to grasp the fact that less than one percent of our global population exercises tremendous control over our politicians and our political systems, regardless of which party you so valiantly support. The rich own and control the banks, militaries, intelligence agencies, and media. If the war machine wants to sell weapons and big oil wants control of your oilfield, the "us versus them" story will be created and the media will once again be selling Joe on Main Street a war that is "necessary due to national security and to preserve the American way of life", blah, blah, blah.

The ego hates the truth, and the truth is this: our leadership is focused on the profits created by conflict. Our leaders don't care about the ensuing destruction or loss of life on either side. The only role Joe on Main Street gets to play in the reality show referred to as "freedom and democracy" is paying the bill.

As a result of Uncle Sam's binge, the United States has become the wealthiest, most powerful nation on the planet, for one simple reason: its corporate and political leadership has, through political, economic, and military means, systematically stolen much of the world's wealth. Motivated by fear, greed, and the desire for power, the corporate and political leadership of the USA will never have enough of what they think they want. The central banking system created by the wealthy in the west has come to control much of the global economy, and today, the wealthy are moving to create a central bank digital currency which will place not only the nation's economy, but also every aspect of your personal financial situation, under the control of the rich.

George Orwell must be rolling in his grave.

Uncle Sam has been drunk for a very long time, and the wreckage is significant. The heroic stories we have all heard a thousand times over do not match the bloody reality that has been perpetrated on the people of the world. And guess what? Uncle Sam still wants more. He cares nothing about the wellbeing of his neighbours and cares little more about the members of his own family. He rules with fear, and his greed and desire for power has created a need for *more* that will never be satisfied.

The proof is there for all to see. As you stand there with one hand over your heart, I ask if you are willing to move the other hand — the one covering your eyes.

Can we continue to give free rein to the egos of small men who are drunk on fear, greed, and desire for power? Can we not see that their need for *more* is insatiable? Will they ever have enough? Ask yourself, in what direction are they taking us? What kind of world will be left for our grandchildren? Can we continue as we have? Are we desperate enough yet?

We, the people of the world, stand at a turning point, and it is time to honestly face the unpleasant truth about who and what we are.

You have a choice. You may feel powerless, but I assure you that you are not alone. There are millions — perhaps billions — of people in our world who feel the same way. Do we continue this downward spiral of insanity, or can you see that if we are to evolve and move past the madness, the only real solution lies in choosing differently?

Choose love. Send Uncle Sam to rehab.

6

Everybody Knows

WHEN I CONSIDER EVERYTHING THAT I have experienced and researched over the last two decades, nothing has been more educational than the discussions I've had with the people I've met along the way. Like the jobs I was sent to, none of these meetings were planned, and, on the surface, they appear to be coincidental. However, as my friends in recovery continue to point out, there are no coincidences. Nothing happens in this world by chance.

It would be easy to bombard you with "he said, she said" stories. There are many. Instead, I'm going to restrain myself and only tell you three of the most remarkable ones.

I will also add that it does not matter to me if you believe anything I have stated within these pages. Again, my goal is not to convince you of anything, though I do hope, despite the cultural influences you have been exposed to throughout your life, that you will develop the courage and the willingness to seriously question the story you've been told about the world that we live in and to search for a greater truth. The story behind the story is almost always there, and it's almost always a much different version than the one conveyed by the talking heads in the media.

My first story is this:

"Tom" worked overseas for the American government. I met him during my travels, and I can assure you that he was in a position to know, beyond all doubt, what he ultimately shared with me and what I am about to share with you.

Tom and I had already discussed numerous events that were taking place in various nations throughout the Middle East when he stated, "The three primary goals of the US military are to sell weapons, control oil, and control drugs."

"What about freedom and democracy?" I asked, my sarcasm getting the better of me.

At that, Tom burst out laughing. This immediately dispelled the nonsensical belief held by many that the United States was somehow attempting to make things right for the people of the world. I was grateful for Tom's response, and I knew from that moment on that we would have an open and candid conversation.

The weapons industry and the influence these lucrative corporations had in Washington and the Pentagon came up in our conversation. I'd read accounts of how politicians and well-connected bureaucrats in both the UK and America had received commissions from weapons sales, and how these funds were often laundered through the offshore banking system. Many of these banks are in Commonwealth countries where wealthy Brits, supported by the UK government, hold a greater degree of control, making it easier for them to launder funds.

It struck me as highly immoral that these devastating wars just happened to be in the best financial interests of our political leaders. This, however, would also help to explain why peace was rarely even a foreign policy talking point. It also explained how a two-term politician could leave office with millions of dollars in their jeans despite only earning a mediocre salary.

My personal beliefs, supported by my research and personal experience, had led me to conclude that many in Washington, motivated by greed, may have directed the CIA to destabilise nations and create the wars the Pentagon fought, killing tens of thousands in the process.

I considered a hypothetical scenario and did some basic math. While $535 million seems like a lot of money, let's put it into perspective: there is approximately an $800 billion defence budget and five hundred and thirty-five elected officials in Washington. If every year $1 million were given to every single elected official in Washington to support war, we'd arrive at a paltry 0.00067% of the defence budget — a mere grain of sand on a California beach.

I'm not suggesting every elected official has been bought off in this manner, but when we understand how much money is involved, not to mention the level of insanity that is required, in invading nations and killing innocent civilians, what, exactly, would it take to motivate an emotionally stable representative of the people to support such endeavours?

Even chronic alcoholics have more empathy than that.

Tom and I then had a brief discussion about oil. It was obvious that if one was going to create a war to sell weapons, there was no point in killing people who had nothing worth stealing. You might as well make the whole operation worthwhile. These people were soulless, not stupid. I knew Iran had been a very progressive, pro-western nation in post-WWII Asia, but the USA had overthrown Iran's democratically elected government in 1953 because Prime Minister Mossadegh had the apparently misguided notion that Iran's oil belonged to the Iranian people. Similar patterns of war and regime change followed in Iraq and other oil-rich nations throughout the Middle East. It wasn't just the Middle East, though: the citizens of Venezuela, Guatemala, Chile, Ecuador, and Bolivia have also been impacted, as the wealth of their nations has also been targeted by US corporations.

Tom then asked, "Remember when you used to hear all about the Colombian drug cartel every night on the news?"

"Of course," I replied, my thoughts going back to the exploits of Pablo Escobar.

"Well, when was the last time you heard anything about the Colombian drug cartel?"

I thought about it for a few moments. "It's been years now."

"Supply of cocaine dry up?"

"No, of course not. There's as much blow out there as there ever was," I responded, knowing full well the stories I'd heard from those seeking help within the recovery community.

"So why don't you hear about it anymore? And what do you think we want in Afghanistan?"

Nothing in my discussion with Tom had piqued my interest more than the issues related to drugs. There was, after all, an opiate epidemic sweeping through North America, and many of us had tried, often in vain, to help those afflicted. I personally had consoled the parents of several kids who had died due to the opiate crisis.

I returned home after my conversation with Tom motivated to learn more, and it didn't take long for me to stumble upon some interesting information from a very reputable source.

In July 2000, the Taliban authorities banned the cultivation of opium poppies throughout all the areas in Afghanistan under their control. In November/December 2000, reports from Afghanistan suggested the vigorous implementation of the ban by the authorities. Early in February of 2001, UNDCP (the United Nations Drug Control Program) conducted a preassessment survey to determine the degree of compliance with the ban. This was followed by another mission in May 2001, when a delegation of major donors from the UNDCP assessed the main poppy cultivating areas of Afghanistan to evaluate the effectiveness of the ban firsthand. Both the preassessment survey and the UNDCP Donor Mission saw the near total success of the ban in eliminating poppy cultivation in Taliban-controlled areas. This finding has been confirmed by the UN's Annual Opium Poppy Survey.[4]

---

[4] United Nations Office on Drugs and Crime (2001): "United Nations Drug Control Program Afghanistan Annual Opium Poppy Survey 2001". Please see www.unodc.org/pdf/publications/report_2001-10-16_1.pdf

The area under opium poppy cultivation increased by 37% in 2020
The total area under opium poppy cultivation in Afghanistan was estimated at 224,000:hectares (202.000.--246,000) in 2020, which represents an increase of 37% or 61,000 hectares: when compared:to 2019

Figure 1 Opium poppy cultivation in Afghanistan, 1994-2020 (hectares)

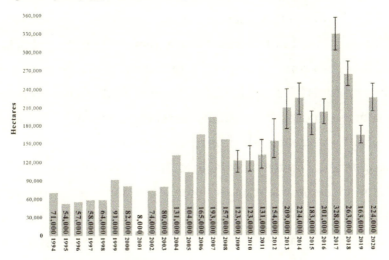

United Nations Office on Drugs and Crime
Afghanistan Opium Poppy Survey 2020[5]

At first glance, what surprised me (because it so starkly contradicted the narrative of the media in North America) was that the bad, bad Taliban had actually banned the cultivation of opium poppies in 2000. The United States' invasion of Afghanistan began in October of 2001 following the ban. Was the timing of that a coincidence? Not according to Tom. As you can see in the above

---

[5] United Nations Office on Drugs and Crime (2020): "Afghanistan Opium Survey 2020: Cultivation and Production – Executive Summary". Please see www.unodc.org/documents/crop-monitoring/Afghanistan/20210503_Executive_summary_Opium_Survey_2020_SMALL.pdf

table, cultivation quickly bounced back from the lows during the 2001 ban and rapidly increased in the years following the US-led invasion.

I find it troubling that the opiate epidemic in North America was preceded by the 2001 Afghan invasion.

Not only that, but it seems the only remedy that the politicians in the USA can come up with for addicts who don't die from drug addiction (which is primarily a mental health and economic problem as opposed to a criminal issue) is incarceration within the corporately controlled, for-profit prison system.

It apparently seems acceptable to those in government that our children at home continue to become the domestic casualties of America's foreign wars, while opportunities to help them are thwarted by the same institutions that created the wars in the first place. I ask myself whether the American government was directly involved or just looking the other way as the drug trade ravaged our streets and took the lives of so many of our children.

I once again feel the need to protect a source and will therefore leave his personal details out of this recount—but there was no grey area in the conversation I had with another person who was intimately involved with US foreign policy. In response to my concerns regarding the opiate epidemic in North America and the well-established fact that Afghan opium had become abundant on our streets following the Afghan invasion, this person confirmed the obvious, stating quite bluntly, "You should see the mansions being built outside of Washington D.C., and everybody knows where the money's coming from." But did *everybody* know? Did Joe and Sally clearly understand how their tax dollars were being used as they stood on Main Street with their hand over their hearts on the Fourth of July? Did the family whose teenage daughter just died with a needle in her arm get the memo?

If *everybody* knew, I had to wonder if the media, military, bankers, and corporate and political leadership were all complicit in the deception. Was it possible that the people whose tax dollars funded the military operations in Afghanistan had been, for two decades and through both a Republican and a Democrat administration, told a story by the mainstream media which consistently avoided what *everybody knows*?

Billions of dollars from the proceeds of opium changed hands during the US-led Afghan invasion. This opens the door to a long list of questions. How were those funds laundered? Were they taxed? How high up the ladder did the corruption go? Was the entire political system owned, ran, and manipulated by a handful of "already wealthy beyond all measure" individuals? Was the ongoing *democratic* process working in the best interests of the people, or was it nothing more than an organised crime syndicate funded by the hardworking taxpayers of the world?

While patrons in coffee shops and bars around the world argued over political points of view, the mainstream media appeared to be as sincere as the promoters of "professional" wrestling, where combatants would hurl insults, and then each other, around the ring for a few minutes and then go drink beer together – all on your nickel.

We've all heard the inflammatory comments thrown back and forth between Democrats and Republicans, but I ask, regardless of which party has held the seat of power, what direction have we been consistently heading in? Isn't it obvious that both parties are governed by major corporate interests? Who, at the end of the day, despite decades of insanity and the immeasurable body count, has ever been held accountable? Rationalised and justified behind a smokescreen packaged and sold as "freedom and democracy", was it really nothing more than a grandiose production — motivated by the fear, greed, and the desire for power of a few — to feed their insatiable need for *more*?

Stop and ask yourself, what is true? Who is currently in a leadership role and *honestly* working for the people? Who among them has a shred of integrity? When the "choice" you are given lies between two corrupt, corporate-sponsored candidates and you see the decent life you are working so hard to create for yourself and your family slipping further and further away, ask yourself, can we continue as we have, or must we change?

Having the courage to honestly look inside is not an easy thing, but there is no easier, softer way. Looking past the story that leads us into insanity and discovering the truth about ourselves is, my dear friends, what recovery and the spiritual transformation Tolle referred to is all about. An alcoholic who chooses to recover must also find the courage to honestly face and accept the truth about who and what he has become. He must realise that he can no longer believe the same lies and deceit his ego once created — the lies he used to rationalise his insane actions. Similarly, we, the global community, can no longer look the other way and deny our role, or the roles played by our respective nations, in the insanity taking place throughout our world. Weapons, oil, and drugs are three of the world's most profitable businesses, and, under the guise of national security, all three have been closely linked to the wars of the last several decades.

I think back to my business trip to Yemen and my realisation that what I was seeing with my own two eyes didn't match the story we'd been told. I had to wonder if the same individuals who profited from these industries not only owned the mainstream media, but also owned and controlled the political process, regardless of which party was in power. Was the media nothing more than the voice of the national ego? Had the mainstream media played a role in rationalising the insanity of our world and, in turn, the loss of millions of lives — the collateral damage brought about by our addiction to war and our need for *more*?

Can we continue as we have?

The final story I wish to share with you comes from yet another "coincidence". (I hope you're smiling and know I'm teasing you every time you see that word.) I was on a small bus heading up into the mountains of a South American country when I just happened to find myself sitting across the aisle from "Mike", an American war correspondent. It wasn't the first time I had met journalists on my travels, but the direct and honest responses offered by Mike were like a breath of fresh air.

I asked Mike where he had worked. As it turned out, we had

travelled similar paths throughout northern Africa and the Middle East. I then asked, "What's it like for you when you go home?"

The response I received was an amused look, as if to say, "What a strange question." Mike's answer was measured: "That's why I live here. I don't go home to America anymore. The people there don't know anything." His response didn't surprise me but left me wondering why, since it was his job to tell the people the story regarding America's wars.

The next question I asked was followed by a hint of a smile from Mike, perhaps caused by a shred of relief that someone else may finally understand. It was, "What does a story you've written look like once it's been published?"

"Like somebody else wrote it," Mike replied.

I didn't ask why his stories were being rewritten. That answer had been obvious since I had first arrived in the Middle East years earlier. It's often said that whoever controls the narrative controls the people. The discussion with Mike caused me to pause and consider the magnitude of the deception, though. I was reminded of how completely convinced I had once been of the stories I had so often told myself; the stories which had kept me locked in my own insanity.

Today, I know beyond all doubt that nothing could have possibly changed in my world until I stopped blaming others and accepted the truth about myself and my actions. It really wasn't any more complicated than that. All that was required was the courage to honestly do so.

Here is the truth: It matters, what you do at war. It matters more than you ever want to know. Because countries, like people, have collective consciences and memories and souls, and the violence we deliver in the name of our nation is pooled like sickly tar at the bottom of who we are. The soldiers who don't die for us come home again. They bring with them the killers they became on our national behalf, and sit with their polluted memories and broken emotions in our homes and schools and temples. We may wish it were not so, but action amounts to identity. We become what we do. You can tell yourself all the stories you want, but you can't leave your actions over there. You can't build a wall and expect to live on the other side of memory. All of that poison seeps back into our soil.[6]

Every Man in This Village Is a Liar by Megan Stack is one of the best books I've ever read. Stack travelled extensively throughout the Middle East as a foreign correspondent, and she reveals to the reader what life was like for the citizens of many countries as America's ego dropped bombs throughout. Stack's perspective is very similar to that which I developed in my own travels. The quote I shared just now accurately summarises the damage done, at a deep level, within our societies as the ego attempts to satisfy its need for *more*.

---

[6] Stack, M.K. (2010): *Every Man in This Village Is a Liar* (p. 51). Anchor Books (eBook).

We are what we do.

The one thing my alcoholism has taught me is that it is impossible for me to become a better human being by harming others. Accordingly, it would also hold true that we can never become a better nation by harming others. When those who profit from weapons, oil, and drugs also own and control the political system and the media, what will the agenda of the nation be? What kind of insanity will prevail under these circumstances? Mass shootings, racism, inequality, corruption, religious extremism, and a lack of integrity within the political system seem to be the natural outcomes when the ego is in charge. Has poison seeped into our soil? Is it already too late? While the citizens in the west are being told their leadership is facing down terrorism, the undeniable truth is that terrorism is being fostered and wars are being *created*, to sell weapons and to control the world's most valuable natural resources — primarily, oil and drugs. Those leading the charge are incredibly wealthy, and they don't want just more; they want it *all*. They run on ego, and the hallmarks of fear, greed, and desire for power are blatantly clear for all to see — if you have the courage to honestly look.

War is nothing new. It is a soul sickness, and its insanity has been repeated by mankind over and over for centuries. We, the people, seem reluctant to learn the lessons history is trying to teach us. I ask you, is the USA addicted to war? If so, we must see the futility in continuing as we have. As with any addiction, the insanity will not stop until we, the people, clearly understand and decide that it *must* stop if we are to evolve and survive.

Is the corporate and political leadership of the United States the only culprit? Of course not—but it still must be said that while the leadership in the USA speaks of freedom and democracy, no other nation has proven to be so committed to claiming the destructive proceeds of war, nor to dominating the rest of the world. America speaks of freedom while destroying any hope of the world's people actually being free. America speaks of democracy while crushing any nation that chooses to chart its own course, especially if it has valuable natural resources.

None of this is complicated, *if* you have the courage to look with open eyes. Many will attempt to rationalise and justify America's actions, but you, I, and most of the world already know that we cannot continue as we have. We are what we do, and any attempt to rationalise insanity is, in itself, insane.

Over the past several decades, the common denominator in much of the world's violence has been the United States and its accomplices. Under the guise of freedom and democracy lies a long list of nations whose governments have been overthrown and replaced by puppets and, in many cases, dictatorships that are more favourable to the corporate and political whims of the west. Then, there are the economic sanctions which are in themselves an act of war. Here, nations are forced to live without the necessities of life while the USA attempts to economically dominate them and force them to comply with their wishes.

North American citizens fail to understand the depths of this insanity because the corporately owned mainstream media (the voice of the ego) rarely provides an honest account of exactly what

America's involvement is. Anyone who does provide irrefutable proof of America's crimes, such as Julian Assange or Edward Snowden, is imprisoned or forced into exile, or worse.

> One evening an old Cherokee chief told his grandson the story of the two wolves. He said, "My son, inside all people there lives two wolves who are in a constant battle with each other. One wolf is evil—it is anger, envy, jealousy, sorrow, regret, greed, arrogance, self-pity, guilt, resentment, inferiority, lies, false pride, and superiority. The other wolf is good—it is joy, peace, love, hope, serenity, humility, kindness, benevolence, empathy, generosity, truth, compassion, and faith."
>
> The grandson thought for a moment and then asked, "Which wolf wins?"
>
> The old Cherokee simply replied, "The one you feed."[7]

It is a tremendously painful thing for loved ones to watch an alcoholic or addict self-destruct. I have witnessed emergency room nurses break down and weep as parents scream in anguish after being told their seventeen-year-old child didn't survive the overdose. I've held the hands of mothers who have left their homes to go to work in the morning, to later find their child lying in the backyard, dead from an overdose.

---

[7] *The Story of Two Wolves* (Native American parable). Sourced from www.aidamuluneh.com/the-wolf-you-feed-1

I'm acquainted with a highly intelligent, well-educated person who not so long ago was lauded by his peers and held a significant position in the community. I was aware of some struggles he was facing and, as I entered my bank one day, I witnessed him in a rage as he pounded and screamed at an ATM that didn't want to give him twenty dollars. Embarrassed upon seeing me, he restrained himself and explained that he needed a bus fare. By this point, he had drunk away his job and his family, and he was drinking away the little bit of his life he had left. I handed him twenty dollars, and he mumbled something about paying me back. I haven't seen him since.

Those of us who have lived with chronic alcoholics or addicts struggle to understand why anyone would act in such an insane manner; why they do it over and over and over again. What are they thinking? Many have no idea. Addicts and alcoholics in recovery will often tell you they have a disease that tells them they don't have a disease; that they just need more of whatever it is they *think* they want. The ego steps in and rationalises their behaviour, thereby making their insanity perfectly acceptable in their own eyes.

To live with an addict is one thing. To place them in leadership roles and hand them a blank cheque year after year, with the expectation of them doing what is in the best interests of others, is beyond comprehension.

I must ask, what is wrong with us? Why would we, the people, continue to support such a destructive way of life?

War is insane. Almost all those who have been lucky enough to come home from it have been telling us that since the beginning of time. We know and understand the destruction it brings to ourselves and others. So, why do we continue to do it? It seems incomprehensible — until you are willing to honestly see and accept the motivating forces of fear, greed, and desire for power that live at the root of it.

If it has become obvious that we, as individuals, all have an ego, is it also conceivable that we, as families, communities, and nations, can also have a collective ego? If so, what are the results when millions of individuals are born into a society where the characteristics of fear, greed, and desire for power — the need for *more* — comprise major aspects of the national identity? What is the result when our egos, left unchecked, run the show?

The destruction our world has seen is stupendous. Millions have died and millions have been left homeless, their lives and communities destroyed. Again, "Either you are with us, or you are with the terrorists," were the words uttered by George W. Bush during the buildup of the invasion of Afghanistan in 2001 — a war, like many of the others, that we now know was based on a long list of lies and fictional intelligence. I wonder how many people in North America would truly value the results of an election if our friends and neighbours from around the world were to cast a vote regarding who they believe the *real* terrorists are.

We are what we do.

What kind of thinking motivated the only nation in history to ever use nuclear weapons not once, but twice? As I've travelled much of the world and surveyed the damage done since, I am troubled by the fact that this same nation wants to dominate every aspect of life within our world. Does this sound like freedom to you?

7

There Is a Solution

WHAT HAS FOLLOWING A SPIRITUAL path as I've travelled all over the world taught me?

It's been over thirty years since I sat on the back steps of the Larsen House Detox Centre and, with some serious reservations, asked the Power of the Universe to take away my obsession with alcohol. I stood at a turning point, and I knew beyond all doubt that there would be dire consequences if I continued to live as I had been. Taking an honest look at who and what I had become wasn't easy, but I could no longer deny the fact that my best thinking had brought me, the star quarterback, to the local detox centre not once, but twice.

I could no longer convince myself that my actions were someone else's fault. To be sure, there had been times when others had made an error, but the truth that began to unfold in front of me was that

I had no control over the actions of others. A pattern emerged, and I began to see that my attempts to control others, whether at home or on the job, were a fundamental aspect of the problematic relationships I'd had. Blaming others for my actions suddenly seemed irresponsible and childish, and it became necessary for me to accept responsibility for my part in the wreckage of my past. It was humbling to clearly see that the story I had been telling myself and others for years was nothing more than an attempt to rationalise my own insanity. The truth, which was now becoming more and more obvious, was that doing things my way was killing me and hurting those I loved.

Love had opened the door a crack. If I wanted to become the world's greatest grandpa, something had to change, and, while I hated to admit it, that "something" was me.

I smile to myself as I write this.

From that depressing, demoralising point in my life, the choice I was now confronted with came right down to this: did I want to live, or did I want to die?

Love won — and I am so grateful, all these years later, to be the (self-proclaimed) greatest great-grandfather in the world.

The past thirty years bear no resemblance to the first thirty-seven of my life. I've been given a brand-new life — one that is far beyond anything I could have ever imagined. And I am not alone in this. By embracing a few spiritual principles, millions of others all over the world (one person at a time) have shared in similar transformations. Out of all the things I have learned in recovery, one main message is clear: change, on a massive scale, is possible.

It is not an overnight matter, but once we clearly accept that we can no longer continue as we have, our grandchildren and great-grandchildren will be grateful that we found the courage to at least, one day at a time, make a new beginning.

Anyone can pick up a gun or a bottle, but finding the courage to honestly look deep inside and ask myself some very difficult questions was one of the most frightening and (at the same time) rewarding things I have ever done. As I began to see the futility of living as I had and made the decision to embrace the spiritual principles of patience, kindness, tolerance, and love, so many of the problems that had been prevalent in my life simply disappeared.

Tolle suggests that we cannot effectively change our outer reality without changing our inner reality, and I concur. My insane and occasionally violent behaviour was a direct result of my fear, selfishness (greed), and need to control (desire for power), all of which were rooted in my ego. I wanted to play God. I wanted everything and everyone in my world to march to my tune. My need for *more* of everything I thought I wanted was insatiable. I wanted to run the world even though I couldn't even manage my own life.

So, what happens when our governments are owned, operated, and controlled by corporate and political leaders who also primarily function through their ego? What transpires when decisions that impact millions of people are made by those who are motivated by a need for *more*, and who function from a mindset rooted in fear, greed, and a desire for power? What happens to our world when those same leaders are placed in control of global economies and sophisticated armies and are no longer accountable to anyone? What is the result when, drunk on power and operating with a bottomless budget (courtesy of the taxpayers), they fail to care for the needs of those whose trust they have violated? How can we, the people of the world, ever expect to raise our children in a peaceful world when those we entrust to lead profit from the wars they themselves create?

You can wrap it in a flag, but insanity is insanity, regardless of how you dress it up.

As you survey the wars, corruption, and racism — the insanity — in our world, ask yourself if we can continue as we have or whether we must change. Is this insanity sustainable? You know, deep down inside, what is true. Listen to the whispers of your own soul. This is a simple process but it most certainly isn't easy, especially in the beginning. As an alcoholic, I spent years trying to avoid what I knew deep down inside to be true about myself. Still, how *you* think — what *you* believe — *is* critical in this worldly transformation. I encourage you to find the courage to sit quietly, listen to your own heart, and recognise that we — humanity — must change.

The only way this can have a lasting effect for generations to come is if the change comes from the bottom up, one person at a time. After all, those who are drunk on power and driven by ego will not suddenly come to their senses. We, the people of this world, do not have to accept what is unacceptable. It is up to us to create a new world — the world we all know we must create. The search for solutions continues to bring me back, again and again, to this same basic understanding: the creation of a sane and peaceful world begins with each of us developing the willingness to honestly see and accept what serves that endeavour and what does not. Which wolf do we feed? Are our thoughts rooted in fear, greed, and the desire for power, or are we focused on being of service to our fellow man?

It really isn't any more complicated than that, and if anyone has a better solution, I would like to hear it. For now, I am convinced that love is not only the easier, softer way, but also the only way.

Tolle refers to the ego as "the blueprint for dysfunction that every human being carries within". We all have an ego and we all have a soul, and I am convinced that deep, deep down inside, even the most insane of us knows the difference between right and wrong. It is still mind-boggling to me that we can refer to the perpetrator in a school shooting as a psychopath while hailing those who have killed countless innocent, unarmed civilians in a long list of orchestrated wars as heroes. The consistent reality is this: the ego will go to great lengths to rationalise and justify its actions, and it will avoid the truth at all costs. Evidence of our national ego's distaste for the truth is obvious. Journalists such as Julian Assange have been imprisoned, and former NSA contractor Edward Snowden lives in exile in Russia, for nothing more than having the courage to tell the world the truth regarding the actions of *our* ego-based publicly funded governments.

Truth, in a democracy, is paramount. But how do we, the people, do our job in holding our leaders accountable and create a sane, sustainable world for future generations when there is such a concerted effort by our leadership to mislead the public? Why do we, the people, allow such insanity to unfold and say nothing? What is wrong with us?

We learn in recovery that developing a spiritual life provides us with a sense of balance that is necessary if we are to cope with the extreme insanity of our egos. We learn, one person at a time, that we don't need to drink the rent money, drive drunk, or beat our spouse. We slowly learn how to step out of the insanity of our egos and into a life where love and service to our fellow man takes centre stage. One person at a time, one day at a time, we discover that change is possible because we have seen it in others. We learn that our need to control only alienates others and we stop doing what we know, deep down inside, doesn't work.

It was early in my recovery that I first heard the expression "the elephant in the room", and it was like being hit on the head with yet another brick. It immediately put into proper perspective the self-deception which had, for two long, miserable decades, become an integral part of my life. It's one thing to deceive others, but I'm somewhat embarrassed today to look back and accept that I spent such a significant portion of my life walking around that elephant and concocting an entire belief system denying its very existence. My denial, combined with my ability to rationalise and justify my destructive behaviour (while blaming others for the circumstances of my life), meant I no longer needed to hold myself accountable, because nothing was ever my fault.

Once I recognised the extent of my self-deception, I realised how pervasive my insanity had become, exemplified by the extensive wreckage of my past.

Have you ever heard an American president step in front of the camera and state, unequivocally, that he was wrong? That he made a mistake, or an error in judgement? Have you ever heard him tell the world, in graphic detail, what America's role was in creating any of the world's problems? Neither have I. Yet nothing has been more beneficial in my life than me clearly and honestly accepting the truth regarding my own insanity. I had to own it. It was humbling to accept that it was *my* alcoholism, rooted in *my* ego, that had stood in the way of *my* growing up. It was *my* alcoholism that had destroyed *my* relationships with loved ones, and it was *my* alcoholism that had made the possibility of *my* forming a true partnership with another human being all but impossible. Regardless of the wrongs others may have committed, I could no longer deny *my* role in the events of *my* past and that it had been *my* ego driving the bus.

Having the willingness to honestly see things as they were led to a revelation. For years, I had lived with the fear that I wouldn't get what I wanted, but the truth was that all I had ever really wanted was more to drink. Deep down, I was terrified to think that someone might see who and what I *really* was. However, it was delusional for me to believe that I could drink myself into insanity *and* convince myself that nobody else knew about it.

The interesting thing about living a life in line with spiritual principles is that it is really simple. You can call me a dreamer, but I've actually come to believe that with a little practice, even a congressman could grasp this spiritual design for living. Saying that, it would likely mean the end of his career. After all, he could no longer support wars for profit or sell his vote, and he would have to commit to a life of service to others, not just the corporate grifters who funded his campaign. (FYI, living a spiritual life does not mean we can't have a sense of humour.)

I leave you here with one main message: I came to recovery full of resentment and angry with the world. Today, I fully realise that the real issue is not liberal or conservative, Democrat or Republican; it is not Muslim, or Hindu, or Christian; it is not Russian, Chinese, Latino, or Palestinian. I am convinced, beyond all doubt, that the one major issue that impedes our ability to evolve, and that can only effectively be dealt with courtesy of a spiritual transformation, is the blueprint for dysfunction that every human being carries within: the ego.

We, the people of the world, stand at a turning point. We've come too far to turn back. It is only by working together in the spirit of love and tolerance that we can overcome the obstacles that the ego has put in our path.

This spiritual process is teachable. By sharing our experience, strength, and hope with each other, we can chart a new course and evolve in peace. Perhaps the only real question you need to ask yourself is, are you desperate enough yet?

Miracles can happen. I've witnessed them in my own life and in the lives of countless others. Left to my own devices, I was powerless, but together, we are not; we are simply in need of a design for living that works. Maybe, just maybe, the recipe required for all of us to move past the insanity and make a new beginning has been provided by none other than a Group Of Drunks.

A man who lies to himself, and believes his own lies, becomes unable to recognise truth, either in himself or in anyone else, and he ends up losing respect for himself and for others. When he has no respect for anyone, he can no longer love, and in him, he yields to his impulses, indulges in the lowest form of pleasure, and behaves in the end like an animal in satisfying his vices. And it all comes from lying — to others and to yourself.

—Fyodor Dostoevsky

8

It's Up to You

SOMEWHERE AROUND FIVE HUNDRED YEARS ago, several nations in Europe began sailing around the world in pursuit of more. They were looking for more fur, fish, spices, gold… more of anything of value.

In North America, they discovered land — and lots of it.

At the time, there were millions of people living in poverty in Europe. Many were being persecuted for their religious beliefs and others were simply being oppressed by the aristocracy, who coincidentally owned and controlled practically all aspects of life under the archaic feudal system. As the seeds of democracy were being sown in North America, many from Europe crossed the Atlantic to embrace freedom and to escape the controlling nature of the European aristocracy.

We've already covered this, but this is where the insane pattern of the ego becomes unmistakably obvious:

As the population in North America grew, the *need for more* land increased. Fueled by the gold rush, the settlement of the west added to this demand. This led to the genocide of the Indigenous people throughout the Americas, with an estimated death toll of fifty-five million people. Men (mostly of European descent) killed millions of Indigenous people and stole the land they had called home for centuries. Those who survived were forced onto reservations and many of the children were sent to residential schools where they encountered severe physical, emotional, and sexual abuse.

The ego's need for *more* didn't stop there. The slave trade became a major industry in the southern states as millions of Africans were captured, chained, and forced onto ships to America, where they were sold primarily to plantation owners. Every aspect of their lives fell under the control of their white "masters".

Can you see that this pattern is still prevalent today? The corporate and political leadership in the west denounces anyone who stands in the way of their need for *more* as terrorists. They speak of freedom and democracy while their own actions exemplify terrorism and consistently lead to the destruction of nations, the loss of freedom, the end of democracy, and the deaths of millions of people.

Can you see how our governments, running on ego and in partnership with major corporations, continue to travel the world killing at will and stealing anything of value?

This thing called "capitalism" hasn't *turned* predatory; it's always been predatory. It has also never worked, nor will it ever work, until we decide to address the dysfunction that every human being carries within: the ego. We in the west consistently demonise Hitler and Stalin, who collectively killed millions, while rationalising our own actions and refusing to see our own hypocrisy.

It should once again be stated that we have little control over the actions of others. Our primary objective, if we are going to live according to spiritual principles, should be to focus on what *we* could do better ourselves. Still, if you're curious about the fallout of America's military escapades, a simple Google check reveals that the USA, during the two hundred and twenty-eight years it has been actively at war for since it officially became a nation in 1776, has killed between twelve and sixteen million people in Korea, Vietnam, and the Middle East alone. Millions more have been displaced. The USA was also instrumental in overthrowing the democratically elected governments in Iran, Chile, and a host of others, and it ultimately established pro-American dictatorships which rarely, if ever, had any interest in taking care of its own citizens. The civil war in Guatemala, for example, began in 1960 due primarily to US foreign policy and lasted for thirty-six years, killing thousands.

The corporate and political leadership in the west is largely responsible for creating the global economic system which has forced the entire world to play this rigged game of Monopoly with them. Whenever it has suited them, they have changed the rules or utilised the military to ensure their need for *more* becomes a reality. It is therefore my contention that America has become the wealthiest nation in the world not because of its own capabilities, but because it has stolen the wealth of the world — primarily from nations who had little or no ability to fight back.

This is the ego at work.

I realise this may be difficult for many to digest. This, however, is my truth based on my research and firsthand experience. You may feel free to believe whatever you wish, but the truth I have come to accept is that America's national ego — the collective force driving the insanity — has no desire for peace. I have no doubt whatsoever that America's military is led by those who are insane and driven by ego. Its need for *more* is insatiable. It will never have enough.

It is humbling to honestly look inside and accept that the greatest enemy we face lives within each and every one of us.

None of this is difficult to understand. If your business is to sell weapons of war, you *need* war in order to do so. Should you have unlimited funding, courtesy of a group of misinformed taxpayers, you are naturally going to focus on creating wars which target other lucrative industries such as oil and drugs.

This pattern is consistent, and mankind has been doing it since time began. However, adding nuclear weapons to the mix makes the situation significantly more insane.

The question, of course, is, can we continue as we have?

The ego is cunning, baffling, and powerful, and I continue to be amused when an all-too-frequent shred of insanity rolls through my own mind. It is in those moments when I can clearly see how easy it is to be led back down the wrong path (especially in the aftermath of traumatic situations) that I am once again reminded that I have a choice in how I respond to the events of my world.

This leads to one aspect of our culture that is near and dear to me:

Trauma is nearly always a precursor to substance abuse addiction. For over twenty years, beginning at thirteen years old, I used alcohol to medicate myself simply because it worked. Booze prevented me from feeling the deep pain surrounding the death of my sister. Today, I know that finding the courage to *feel* that pain was necessary for me to heal. It wasn't easy, but there was no easier, softer way. It is often painful to look at the truth within us and our world, but it is always worth it.

Indigenous people and African American communities, courtesy of the fear, greed, and desire for power rooted in the egos of our European forefathers, have suffered (and continue to exhibit) generational trauma. Genocide, residential schools, slavery, inequality, racism, and poverty, complete with all the physical, sexual, mental, and emotional abuse forced upon those communities, has led to their significant representation within the recovery community and in the prison population. A majority of those incarcerated have been imprisoned due to their involvement with drugs or alcohol. Our current lawmakers, many of whom are descendants of the corporate and political leadership that was directly involved in creating these problems to begin with, continue to use force to deal with what is a mental health issue.

Substance abuse addiction is a health issue, not a criminal one. If you follow the money (ego), you will discover that our corporate for-profit prisons are full of Black and Indigenous people who are trying to deal with the pain created by a system imposed on them by their jailers. Many of those who don't make it to prison are dying due to the garbage found in uncontrolled street drugs.

We must follow Portugal's example here. Two decades ago, Portugal's drug problem was one of the worst in Europe, and their prisons were overrun with those who had been locked up for drug related offences. In response, the leadership was wise enough (or soulful enough) to legalise all drugs. Addicts were then provided with clean, pharmaceutical grade drugs at no cost, which were prescribed by medical professionals. As a result, the stigma attached to being an addict has been greatly reduced in Portugal. People are no longer dying in the alleys due to overdose or bad drugs, and because the drugs are clean, there are limited health issues related to their use. The "junkies" are now working and paying taxes, which has led to a reduction in drug related crime. They didn't stop there. The Portuguese government took the money that had been spent on the prisons and reallocated it to rehab and counselling services for addicts.

In the twenty years since, Portugal has gone from having one of the worst drug problems in Europe to being a model for the rest of the world. The illicit drug trade has all but disappeared, and those directly impacted are receiving the help they need, instead of the punishment that only added to the trauma that led to the problem in the first place.

Doing the right thing because it is the *right* thing to do (not the most convenient or the most profitable thing) changes our world. We live in a global community, and by embracing the spiritual solution with a goal of being of service to mankind, we begin, one person at a time, to make the world a better place for the majority of the earth's inhabitants. However, in this current ruthless game of Monopoly, someone must lose for others to win. But why do we even play their game when we are more than capable of working together to create new lives and a new world?

I believe our grandchildren and great-grandchildren will be confronted with significant issues and deserve to be alleviated from the added burden created by a handful of selfish fools who are drunk on power and have no desire to live in peace.

If the egos of our corporate and political leadership have no desire for peace, I ask you, whose job is it to lobby for such peace? I believe it is ours—yours and mine. I believe the only thing powerful enough to rein in the insanity created by the ego-based leadership of this world is the will of the people.

There is a spiritual revolution sweeping the earth that is likely to be downplayed, if mentioned at all, by the mainstream media. With increasing frequency, people all over the world are beginning to see the reality that we can no longer continue as we have, and that the ego, feeling that its position of power is being threatened, has "ramped up" the insanity. This turmoil has created a much greater awareness among the people of the world regarding exactly who and what the problem is.

As the world awakens to the reality that change is on the way, the ego becomes even more insane in its efforts to remain in charge. All of this makes for a bumpy ride, and the turbulence itself, while difficult to manage, tells us that change is coming. All that is required for individuals to start this journey is the understanding that some kind of change is required, followed by a firm decision to commit to a simple spiritual process — a process rooted in love.

I ask you, is it possible for the global community to overcome the insanity of the ego and create a new world — a soulful, kind, and loving world — in the same manner that millions of drunks, driven by the gift of desperation, have created brand-new lives?

As this transformation continues to unfold, you will come to see that you have a choice in how you respond to these events. If it is obvious to you that violence and the need to control is a function of the ego, does it make sense to respond to the events unfolding in our world in a violent manner?

If we are to escape the insanity of the ego and evolve in love, our behaviours must also be rooted in love. Gandhi taught us that "an eye for an eye makes the whole world blind". Significant challenges lie ahead, and they can be solved if we work hand in hand with our global neighbours in the spirit of love and tolerance. This is the only way we will be able to overcome the destructive forces we ourselves have created. We have no control over the actions of other nations, but, as members of a democracy, we, the people, not only have the power but the obligation to hold our own leaders accountable for their acts of insanity.

The corporate elite own and control our governments and our democracies hang in the balance. You may not want to admit it, but that is the elephant in the room. That is the national ego at work, and, left untreated, its addiction to *more* will ultimately kill the host.

Nothing goes in a straight line forever. At some point, things either self-destruct or we learn from our past and make changes. We can either ride the garbage truck all the way to the dump or evolve. There is no Plan B.

It's up to you. I cannot decide for you, but I can tell you that you are not alone. The design for living I and millions of others have come to enjoy is simple, but none of it is easy.

I'm not going to argue with the suggestion that ignorance is bliss. Ignorance didn't solve the multitude of problems my ego created. It was only by finding the courage to stop blaming others and to honestly see the truth of my own actions that I was able to heal. And I am not alone. Through that same process, millions of others have also found the courage to heal.

In the years that followed my decision to commit to this design for living, the process of practicing these principles (especially the process of honest self-examination) has become second nature to me. I am not a saint, but I'm prepared to accept responsibility for my actions when they have caused harm to others. I work at forgiving others, and, through that process, I have learned to forgive myself for the things I have done or have failed to do.

It was never my intent to adapt this beautiful design for living to a process through which we can examine the world we live in, but if we can no longer continue as we have, I know of no other process capable of creating change as peacefully or as effectively as these basic recovery principles.

We must decide to work with our global neighbours, not dominate and control them. We must stop the wars, learn from history, and evolve in a spirit of love and tolerance. My grandchildren and my great-grandchildren deserve it, and so do yours.

My dear friend Alex tells me that man's propensity to destroy others, himself, and his planet is the result of human nature, and on that point we agree. Alex goes on to suggest that human nature can't be changed, and that is where I'm compelled to explain that my human nature had, for years, rendered me a suicidal, out-of-control drunk who was frequently a menace to society, but I've changed, and so have millions of others.

If you believe that we can no longer continue as we have — that some kind of transformation is necessary — I will remind you that, one person at a time, we are changing the world. You have a choice. Which wolf do you wish to feed?

Once we understand and accept the fact that every single issue plaguing our world is manmade, are we not then obligated to ask why we are doing this to ourselves? The wars, the environmental destruction, the corruption, the racism, and the hate we see are all rooted in fear, greed, and desire for power, and are all created by the ego.

The ego rules through fear and has no other choice but to view love as a threat. Therefore, love, in the eyes of the ego, becomes an act of rebellion.

Living from the soul is living with love. Love has provided me with an alternative to the fear, greed, and desire for power that had been at the root of my insanity. Am I cured? Of course not; I still have more than my fair share of fuckedupedness, where my ego jumps behind the wheel and takes me for a ride. But it is getting easier for me to see when I have gone off track. Plus, the destruction I cause these days pales in comparison to the destruction of my past.

I continue to be a work in progress, and I have no expectations of ever becoming perfect.

Conclusion

I have spoken out. I have said my piece. Am I afraid? You bet I am. But I am more afraid of what the future will have in store for the children in my life, should we fail to summon the courage to do what we all know, in the depths of our souls, we must.

Love is the only way out. Love for each other, love for our children, and love for our children's children is how we escape the insanity of our own egos.

I have done my best to shine a light on the path out of the insanity that is being forced upon the people of the world by those currently at the helm of it. Their egos will not appreciate the resistance and any desire for change. As a result, their responses may become increasingly more insane. Will they come for me? Will I be slandered and ridiculed and discredited? Will I be pilloried in the public arena of manufactured news? Will they find a way to put me in the cell Assange only just vacated? Or to torture me in Room 101? Or will they leave me no alternative but to end my days, looking over my shoulder as I sip tea with Snowden in a Moscow café? Will I, too, be "suicided"? Or will they make it much more obvious while at the same time sending the opposite message to the millions who know in their hearts that we simply cannot continue as we have? That things must change?

We have come to a turning point. Change of a significant

proportion is not only necessary, but also unavoidable and *en route*. Fear, greed, and the insatiable desire for power are the hallmarks of man's ego. While the violence perpetrated upon the people of this world may lead to our destruction one hundred times over, love will still be here waiting for you to choose differently. After all, there is no other way.

The war—the real battle—isn't out there; it's inside each and every one of us. You have a choice. Choose love.

Acknowledgements

You Can't Stop Love would not exist today had I not crossed paths with a certain Group Of Drunks — a group of people who had previously found the courage to face the insanity that was at play within their own lives. The realisation that I could no longer continue to live as I had was, by itself, insufficient motivation for me to resolve my own insanity and fully comprehend the imminence of my demise. That Group Of Drunks shared with me the design for living that had already transformed the lives of millions of others. They have loved me back to health, and I will be forever grateful for the gift they have so willingly shared, and continue to share, with me and with the world.

Had you told me thirty-five years ago that the day would come when I would write a book based on a personal commitment of trying do the "right" thing, day in and day out, for no other reason than the fact that it's the right thing to do, I would have ordered another drink and insisted you share with me whatever it was you were smoking. Today, looking back at my life, I realise that my understanding of love — *real love* — developed during my younger years without me ever recognising it. There were two people who provided me with real life examples of love, integrity, and human decency, despite the difficult issues they themselves were forced to face. Having heard the stories of countless addicts and alcoholics (many of whom have suffered trauma far greater than I) and seeing firsthand how most of the world's people live, I am left with nothing but gratitude for the two beautiful souls I am blessed enough to call my parents. If I had to do it all over again I would gladly do it with them.

How could I begin to broach the subject of love without expressing the joy I've come to experience through the relationships I have with my children, my grandchildren, and my great-grandchildren? The motivation that led to my own awakening was a byproduct of that very love, and with every new addition (whether by birth or by marriage), this familial community has evolved into something very special. Becoming the world's greatest grandfather was once my goal, and despite knowing I have often fallen short of that, I have been consistently reminded that it is progress (not perfection) that is the real goal. My son, Craig, who I frequently refer to as the kindest human being on the planet, perhaps said it best when, referring to my global travels, he stated, "As long as we're here, you're going to keep coming back, because we're that impressive." He couldn't be more correct.

I also wish to acknowledge the numerous individuals I have "coincidentally" encountered in my travels who have also contributed to *You Can't Stop Love*. Many of them have been directly involved in shaping the events of our world. Among them are some active and former members of the United States Military and members of the Intelligence Community. Special recognition goes out to the men and women of Veterans for Peace, which, in my opinion, is one of the finest organisations in the world. I would also like to thank S. Brian Willson, Frank Dorrel, Jerry Rubin, and John Perkins, who have all personally shared their experience with me. The late John Pilger, a documentary filmmaker, has long been one of my heroes, as has Chris Hedges and Edward Snowden. All these people have steadfastly worked to show us the truth. Nobody, however, deserves to be recognised more for their commitment to the people of this world than Julian Assange, who was incarcerated by the corrupt egos of this world for no other reason than having the courage to tell us the truth. Assange clearly understands that both democracy and change relies upon our ability to be rigorously honest about who and what we are.

Looking back at my life there was one shining example of a man who, with incredible honesty, made it fun to look at ourselves with honesty. Perhaps it is something that comes with age and an understanding that the road gets narrower as we make our way toward the end of our lives. The fear of what others may think dissipates as we settle into the truth of who and what we are. During the last few years of his life, comedian George Carlin nailed it. While it's been several years since his passing, he saw, with incredible clarity, the direction we were travelling in. He was a great teacher, and he told us the truth about our society, our governments, and ourselves — and he did it all with a great sense of humour. There was, however, a price to be paid for his honest critique of the corporate and political leadership in our world, yet despite the negative repercussions, he stayed true to who he was. He did not sell out. We need more like him.

I believe it is absolutely necessary to thank Hayley and the staff at Onyx Publishing for their commitment and professionalism in bringing this particular aspect of this project to fruition. I say "this particular aspect" because I've often viewed this book as a good place to start, and while there is much more work to do, I have come to believe that right from the very beginning, the staff at Onyx have recognised and shared this vision. It has been a privilege and a joy to work with you all. Thank you so much.

You Can't Stop Love
Is Going Global

We, the people of the world, stand at a turning point. We ask for your support and invite you to share your experience, strength, and hope for the future by joining the *You Can't Stop Love* global community. Simply scan the QR code below to be taken directly to youcantstop.love, where you will discover friends you've never met before as we, along with our global neighbors, restore our world to sanity, one person at a time.

About the Author

John Fast is a father, grandfather, and-great grandfather. His work in the oil and gas sector has taken him all over the world, including several years in various countries throughout the Middle East. His fields of study include international politics, history, and conflict resolution, but he contends that his greatest education came from his years of involvement with members of addiction recovery programs.

His books include *You Can't Stop Love* and *The 12 Steps to Peace*. He has also authored a dark comedy screenplay entitled *It's Great Being Me*. All his work focuses on the practical benefits of spiritual transformation. To cite the millions of those in recovery who have personally experienced such a transformation: "If a bunch of drunks can be restored to sanity and become the most loving and peaceful people in the world, why can't we all?"

www.ingramcontent.com/pod-product-compliance
Lightning Source LLC
Jackson TN
JSHW082117290125
78016JS00002B/9

9 781913 206710